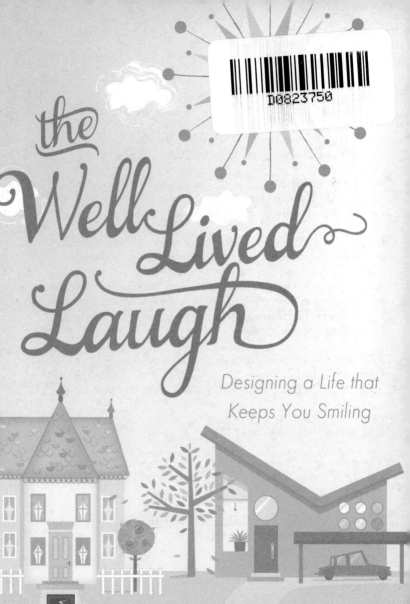

the Well Lived Laugh

Designing a Life that
Keeps You Smiling

BARBOUR

From the Author of *Wake Up Laughing*
Rachel St. John-Gilbert

© 2012 by Rachel St. John-Gilbert

Print ISBN 978-1-61626-726-1

eBook Editions:
Adobe Digital Edition (.epub) 978-1-60742-0378
Kindle and MobiPocket Edition (.prc) 978-1-60742-0392

All rights reserved. No part of this publication may be reproduced or transmitted for commercial purposes, except for brief quotations in printed reviews, without written permission of the publisher.

Churches and other noncommercial interests may reproduce portions of this book without the express written permission of Barbour Publishing, provided that the text does not exceed 500 words and that the text is not material quoted from another publisher. When reproducing text from this book, include the following credit line: "From *The Well-Lived Laugh*, published by Barbour Publishing, Inc. Used by permission."

All scripture quotations in this publication are from *THE MESSAGE*. Copyright © by Eugene H. Peterson 1993, 1994, 1995, 1996, 2000, 2001, 2002. Used by permission of NavPress Publishing Group.

Cover Illustration: Amy Cartwright
Illustration/Deborah Wolfe LTD

The author is represented by WordServe Literary Group, Ltd., Greg Johnson, Literary Agent, 10152 S. Knoll Circle, Highlands Ranch CO 80130

Published by Barbour Publishing, Inc., P.O. Box 719, Uhrichsville, Ohio 44683, www.barbourbooks.com

Our mission is to publish and distribute inspirational products offering exceptional value and biblical encouragement to the masses.

ᏇᏇᎻᎪ Member of the
Evangelical Christian
Publishers Association

Printed in the United States of America

Dedication

To Laura Jacobs—a foxhole friend. Thanks for being an easy laugher and tight hugger, and for *showing* me a thing or two about grace. I still can't wrap my head around it, but how you've treated me over these eight years has brought me closer than I've ever been before. I always feel closer to Jesus and better about myself after spending time with you. I am so grateful that God gave you the capacity to handle eccentricity.

Contents

Introduction:
Don't Tell Me
What to Do

I don't know about you, but I don't like to be told what to do.

Or how to feel.

Or what to think.

After talking with other women, one thing becomes clear to me: many of us haven't outgrown the preschool phase when we were anxious to become big kids but had to keep fending off would-be helpers with a jagged graham cracker while warning, "I do it *myself* !"

In a culture in which we are constantly bombarded with what *other* people do, feel, and think via the Internet, television, books, and radio, it's easy to feel disconnected from our own point of view or. . .perspective.

And that can leave us feeling like little kids on the cusp of Big Kiddom, still having our coats zipped up by the teacher, waaay past the Adam's apple, when we have a pretty good idea how to zip them up ourselves, comfortably midchest, if we just had the chance. This book is about providing that chance—a chance to reconnect with our own unique perspective. Or zip up our own zippers, if you please.

What exactly does *perspective* mean? The word has Latin origins related to "sight." For the purpose of our discussion here (and since I'm the one doing the typing), I'll define perspective simply as "the filter that determines how we see things."

For example, let's suppose that at some time in your life, your children convince you, against your better judgment to, say, ride the Scrambler at the state fair of Texas, the timing of the request being most inopportune, seeing as how you were coerced by the same offspring just moments before to sample a concoction called "fried bubblegum" (you can't make this stuff up—but some enterprising vendor sure did). Having no backbone to speak of, you decide to humor the kids, and by so doing, end up spewing a regurgitated version of the aforementioned confection onto nearby passengers. This is precisely the kind of scenario in which you will no doubt have developed a new perspective.

Here's one way your personal filter might determine how you view the consumption of fried sweets mixed with frenetic motion in the future:

1) Gum is meant to be chewed, not battered and deep-fried.
2) Never give in to the impassioned pleas of children on a sugar high.
3) "The Scrambler" is not just a catchy name— it's the violent fate of the contents of your stomach.

So next year when the state fair comes around and your children are hopping around you like Chihuahua puppies, hyped up on fried cotton candy and begging you to ride the Scrambler, you will have the benefit of perspective to help you politely but firmly respond, "Put a lid on it."

This is often how we develop perspective—through our experiences, both positive and negative. But other factors influence how we see things, as well: the family we grew up in, the part of the country we come from, our personality, our theology, our philosophy, and a host of other things. For many of us, perhaps the most important influence on our perspective is our Judeo-Christian values. The scriptures offer timeless wisdom that can help us filter out undue pressure and filter in our God-given freedom to make our own choices.

In this age of nonstop marketing in which we're aggressively "persuaded" to purchase a product or sign on to a cause, it's easy to forget that our choices are a precious commodity that shouldn't be easily wrestled away from us. And it's not only marketers who try to influence our choices: people in our social circles, some well-intentioned and some not, often try to persuade us to do something or be someone that may not be right for us. Just because some*one* decides some*thing* is important, it doesn't mean *we* have to follow suit. Following suit is for card games, not the serious business of designing our lives.

The Bible says, "Christ has set us free to live a free life" (Galatians 5:1). If we carelessly forfeit our choices based on someone else's perspective, we may find ourselves feeling like indentured servants to others—or their causes and priorities. And like that kindergarten kid zipped up mummy-tight in a winter coat by the sturdy hands of someone else, we can start to feel hot under the collar. And for good reason. . .

• • • • • • • When Perspective Meets Choice • • • • • •

Our perspective impacts our choices. And every choice we make has a consequence. Here's the kicker: *The sum of our choices defines our lives.* Taking ownership of the filter that determines how we see life is one of the most powerful things we can do for ourselves. Giving up that ownership is one of the most debilitating things we can do to ourselves. Owning our own perspective can be the difference between living a life that's designed to fit or living a life that's one-size-fits-all.

Stephen R. Covey, author of *The 7 Habits of Highly Effective People*, puts it this way:

> *How different our lives are when we really know what is deeply important to us, and, keeping that picture in mind, we manage ourselves each day to be and to do what really matters most.*[1]

Laura Jacobs, a foxhole friend to me and many other women, once told me, "Women tend to live a lot of life inside their heads." She went on to explain that we constantly battle pressures—some *external* (others-imposed), some *internal* (self-imposed)—and spend a great deal of mental and emotional energy trying to tackle those pressures alone. "When we give in to pressures for the wrong reasons, we can find ourselves feeling lost or overwhelmed or even depressed," Laura concluded.

My friend's words struck a chord with me and set my thoughts in motion. "You know, this is where a perspective that is uniquely ours can come in handy. Because the right filter can put a spring in our step in record time; and the wrong filter can make us feel stepped *on* for a very long time."

"True dat!" Laura concurred, with an eloquence

that is uniquely *her.*

A few days later when I joined Laura for a walk, I had a question for to her ponder.

"What if I wrote about some of the pressures that weigh on women's minds, and then encouraged them to *decide for themselves* how to view them?"

Laura clapped her hands together in a "Eureka! We've done it" way, and then mischievously raised one eyebrow as she shot a look my way.

"Perfect," she said slyly.

Psychiatrist and famed author M. Scott Peck has said that a trusted friend who is a good listener can be as helpful to a troubled soul as an expensive therapist. I've often found that to be true. So my hope with this book is that by mulling things over together, we can alleviate some of the pressures we feel (or remove them all together)—and *BAM!*—with a shift in perspective, change our lives for the better. And maybe we can even save ourselves some pricey therapy sessions.

Maybe if we silence the self-defeating monologues that loop in our brains, our lives will become *well-lived* rather than haphazardly endured. A well-lived life, free of unnecessary burdens, leaves more room for laughter and levity—two things that researchers say are key to facing life's challenges with courageous optimism.

The book that you hold in your hands is not a how-to volume, but instead an invitation to consider together some offbeat observations about internal pressures we place on ourselves (like, "Make something of yourself!") and external pressures we hear from others (like, "Eat healthy!"). *Then you can decide how you want to approach those pressures based on a thoughtfully conceived perspective of your own.* After all, not all pressures are bad—some are a catalyst to positive change. But we can get into exhausting head games and emotional turmoil when we yield to another's perspective without giving our own a fighting chance.

There you have it. Now that you know what you're in for, it's time to (a) toss this book like a lit firecracker, (b) clutch it to your breast like a lost puppy, or (c) say to yourself while lighting a candle on a stormy night, "What have I got to lose? The electricity's out again."

Happy people participate
in their own destinies and
forge their own happiness.
They don't wait for events or other
people to make them happy.[2]

DAN BAKER, PH.D.
What Happy People Know

In an instant, a shift in perspective can
change everything.[3]

B. F. JOHNSON

1
The Slowest Loser

❊

The Pressure to Lose Weight

As much as I love food, I don't love from whence it comes.

Grocery shopping is low on my list of want-tos, though I admit that the advent of in-store coffee bars has moved G-Day up a few notches. A triple shot of espresso can have me happily zipping about the aisles, filling my cart with a flourish. Though often, by the time I reach the checkout counter, I don't recognize most of the items I am loading onto the conveyor belt. But I had a nice time.

On one such excursion, I overheard a conversation between two women who were just out of my line of sight. One voice said excitedly, "I was really good over the weekend. When we went to Fuzzy Taco, I only ordered a chicken taco and a side salad. It's so hard, but I'm getting close to my goal weight."

The other voice squealed with approval, "Ohhh, I'm so proud of you!"

Being a struggling dieter myself, I tried to catch an inconspicuous glimpse of the accountability partners to see how "close to goal weight" might look. When I spied the ladies, I thought, *That can't be right.* Both were thin and fit—the last body types you'd expect to hear discussing portion control. As I surveyed the sleek physique of the voice of Lone Taco, I whispered to myself in disbelief, "Your goal weight is my birth weight." Okay, maybe her goal weight was closer to what I weighed in sixth grade, but still. . . .

Apparently weight loss is an arena of modern life where there are many different perspectives. To give credit where it's certainly due, I can almost guarantee that if you ask a fit friend how she stays trim, she will tell you that she has an eating and exercise plan. The difference between these women and the more padded masses? They actually work their plan. They live the adage "No pain, no gain." To which I say, "Nuts!" Which is the only four-letter word I'm allowed to write without risking repercussions.

• • • • • • • • • • • • • That's Heavy, Man • • • • • • • • • • •

After three pregnancies that left a tenderloin of fat implanted around my waist and hail damage on my thighs, I would so love to have been given a celestial gimme on body type. One only has to look from a thoroughbred foal to a baby elephant to realize that even some in the animal kingdom get a hereditary leg up when it comes to being born with an attractive form. Even so, these blessed ones—whether horse or heroine—can't remain svelte by lying under a shade tree and cozying up to a box of Ho-Hos all afternoon.

I'm happy to report that I'm now on the backside of having worked forty pounds off my backside. That may sound admirable to some, and less so to those of you who have lost a lot more than that. What may be somewhat unusual about this achievement is that it's taken me two years to do it. I'm not The Biggest Loser, but I'm likely The Slowest Loser. And if someone makes a killing by producing a reality TV show on this concept, I will need to add more faux expletives to my vocabulary. "Nuts!" will be woefully inadequate.

My major hindrance to expeditious pound-dropping is that, oddly enough, I really love the taste of food. And I love variety. So one of my strategies to surviving the whole dieting ordeal was finding or developing what I call "twin foods." Like Ado Annie in the musical *Oklahoma!,* who "Cain't say no," I really don't like to say no. I know, I know, I'm losing some of you "no pain, no gain" people the longer I stay on this circuitous rabbit trail. But hey, not everyone loves pain the way you guys do. And if there is a way for pain weenies to lose weight, who better than I to lead the way?

Because of my contentious relationship with *no,* I hoped that dieting might not *feel* like dieting if I created a counterfeit food for every delicious one I had to give up or eat in micro portions.

So for a long while now, I've been tackling my eating demons on my own terms—in a somewhat creative way involving twin foods. For example, I might say to myself, "Gee, a big bowl of banana pudding sure sounds good right about now." But instead of the real stuff, I'd get a small bowl, drop in a ripe, chopped banana, some flax meal, and fat-free whipped cream. Okay, so it's taken me two years to lose forty pounds this way, but I now possess an impressive weaponry of twin foods in my eating arsenal. While these foods are not identical twins (for obvious reasons), they are healthy "fraternal alternatives" that have helped me create a culinary world where I can nurture my rebellious streak by saying yes more than no. And I like that. A lot.

· · · · · · · · · · · Wanted: Motivation · · · · · · · · · · ·

Backing up a bit, before I was able to muster the motivation to change the way I ate and get my body moving, I was sooo tempted to take a shortcut. After months of surveying my unwanted lumps and sags and watching the scale display increasingly alarming numbers, I began to envy my neighbor. She covers every square inch of her body with a stylish, floor-length dress that is characteristic of her native India. Talk about taking the pressure off! What I'd give to say, "Sorry, but it is against my religion to display my physical flaws and fat in public." Ecstasy.

I even thought about paying a seamstress to design seven of these long, flowing tunics for me in bright shades of fuchsia, turquoise, lime, etc.—one for every day of the week. While this would be a relief for me, it is even more tempting to order a set for my preteen daughter. Adolescent hormones kicking in with the neighbor boy? Problem solved.

Of course when one is considering camouflaging techniques to avoid dieting, it's not the best time to take notice of the perkier bodies of the young. During such a time, I was walking around my son's college campus, and I remember being hit with a pang of disbelief when I spied a coed who was cover-girl material. As we stared at Miss Perfect strolling by with a carefree toss of her blond hair and a flash of her snow-white teeth, I remarked to my friend, "She must be from another species."

Truly, in moments when I come face-to-face with movie-star genes, I feel more closely related to, say, a walrus than a perfect specimen of womanhood. I know that sounds self-deprecating, but I happen to have exceptionally nice canine teeth. I'm pretty confident that in a side-by-side-by-side photo comparison of myself in a bikini, Cameron Diaz, and a walrus, the average villager in Papua, New Guinea (or Greenwich for that matter), would conclude that I more closely resemble marine life. That said, I think anthropologists should add a new species to the female race— something like *coveris girlis,* so the pressure's off the rest of us to resemble them in any way, shape, or form.

And can we agree that our problems with our weight loss do not stem from lack of information? If all we needed to be trim was to absorb the tidal wave of data on how to be trim, we'd all fit into Angelina Jolie's sequined gowns. Can't you see it now? You've met your goal weight and you've been chosen to deliver a speech to the Academy of Health: "Oh, thank you, researchers! All I had to do was eat a thousand calories a day and exercise six days a week. How I wish I'd known sooner."

The crux of the issue lies more with lack of motivation than lack of information. What motivated me to get moving and change my eating habits? After seeing photos of my puffy body, I realized I was beginning to resemble the Michelin Man. In case you're wondering, I was less concerned about the *man* part than I was the inner-tubey business.

I knew where I was headed wasn't going to be pretty if I didn't apply the brakes. Like the kid on a raft who gets pulled away with the tide, I was going to find myself at the wrong resort if I didn't start paddling my way back. At first, I tried positive self-talk, asking, "How amazing would it be to swear off spandex and be able to jog with my daughters?" Well, the answer to that question was a resounding, "Pretty awesome!" You'd think that would be motivation enough. But then I realized it would take months, maybe even *years* of daily choices that went against my love of food and penchant for telling myself yes.

Dang.

Faced with the reality that there would be no quick-fix cowboy saddling up a white horse to rescue me from a future of fiber and sweat, I decided to phone a friend. Providentially, my phone-a-friend had been taking some life-coaching classes.

"Rachel," she asked, "can you think of any benefit to this journey taking a long time?"

As soon as the question left her lips, I knew the answer held power—because I had come to view *time* as my archenemy in this battle of the behind.

"Well," I said with a sigh, "that's a great question. I'm not sure. . ."

I halted and thought a little more.

"I guess for one thing, the longer I do the right things to lose weight, the more likely those *habits* will stick with me rather than *pounds* sticking to me."

"Yeah." My friend murmured knowingly. "I think you're right about that. Can you think of anything else?"

I sat quietly, letting my thoughts solidify. "The longer I have to face challenging situations at home or at restaurants, at the movies or parties, the more I'll have to come up with alternatives I can live with for the rest of my life."

"Bingo." I could hear her smiling. "Changing habits and beating addictions can be some of the hardest challenges we tackle in life. I bet you'll figure out some ways to keep from getting discouraged—try not to worry about how long it's taking."

As you can guess by the length of my journey, I nabbed that last piece of advice like a cheating dieter scarfing down a warm Nestlé Toll House cookie. Slow, I can do. Slow, in fact, is one of my favorite speeds. Eventually, slow and steady helped me build up enough motivational steam to complete my weight-loss marathon.

Interestingly, I recently read of a motivational theory called SDT (Self-Determination Theory) that I wish I'd known about a couple of years ago. [Author's note: Please be careful not to transpose letters on this acronym. Heaven forbid that you should say I recommended a new theory of motivation called STD.] Dicey acronyms aside, the self-determination theory boils down to this: the more we do what we *want* to do rather than being *forced* to do something we don't like, the happier and more successful we tend to be. (Which is the underlying theme of this book, by the way.)

The idea is to find activities and foods that feed your motivation—you like them or you like the results you get from them. For example, in studies where people were most successful in keeping their New Year's resolutions for exercising, they linked that success to three things:

1) Desirable outcome: being healthier, etc.
2) Desirable activity: something you'll do alone
3) Desirable relationships: an engaging buddy

In regard to exercise, the SDT equation looks like this:

$$\text{Desirable Outcome} + \text{Desirable Activity} + \text{Desirable Friend} = \text{Success}$$

In my case, if I had not had two dogs staring at me and whining to be taken on a walk, I may not have ever gotten my caboose on the track during the height of my Michelin-ness. So, I thank God for Spotty and Ginger—and dog-mother guilt. What I couldn't do for myself, I could do for my pets. The more I got myself moving and the happier I saw my dogs, the more I *wanted* to walk every day.

Mercifully, my opera singer friend Jennifer was looking for a walking buddy at that time. I liked the idea of boosting my self-esteem by being seen with the layperson's version of star soprano Renée Fleming—and since Jennifer has a great sense of humor and refreshing insight on everything from motherhood to vocal performance, I was "in."

So on days we might otherwise have been tempted to sleep in, Jenn and I would meet to walk. Most days, time flew as we got lost in our witty repartee (which is testimony to our chatty natures, seeing that we often met at 6:30 a.m.). On other days, we shored up each other's faltering resolve not to cash in our dieting chips for potato chips. We'd express our mind-bending frustrations, dark self-doubts, strategy shifts, and belief that God was "with us still"—always knowing that, sooner or later, we'd be ready to "journey onward," because neither of us wanted to go back to our old lifestyles.

In addition to walking, I took up some resistance weight lifting, which, might I say, I resisted with a passion. "Muscle burns fat," the experts say, so I did the best I could with this activity I hated. I kept hand weights on the edge of the bathtub—the poor man's version of water aerobics.

Some of you Bally Total Fitness people are shaking your heads in disbelief at this very moment. Fine.

But just you wait—when we turn ninety, who is more likely still to be doing their exercise routine? My workout may be low on intensity, but it's high on longevity.

Looking back, I realize I kind of fell into the Self-Determination Theory before I even knew there was such a thing. Actually, I fall into a lot of things. Mostly trouble. But this is how SDT played out for me:

1) Desirable outcome: swearing off spandex,
    jogging with my girls
2) Desirable activity: walking dogs, bathtub
    aerobics
3) Desirable relationships: walking with an
    engaging friend twice a week

I wish I could say, "And the weight just fell off!"
Although if that had been the case, chronic dieters
would no doubt kick this book to the curb and bid it a
hearty "Good riddance!"

No, rest assured, every pound clung to my body
for dear life—though the pounds eventually slid into
oblivion over two years' time. And I'm not off the
hook yet—I would be healthier if I lost more weight
and became even more active. We'll see how that goes,
because I would also like to eat 1,500 calories a day
instead of about 1,200. So I have some thinking to do
and choices to make—and perhaps hardest of all, more
motivation to find.

This lifelong food lover is grateful to God for
helping her with what often felt like an impossible
endeavor. On many days, I felt like a failure—and
wanted to give up more times than I can count. When
I was under an avalanche of discouragement, God kept

bringing this thought to my mind: *You know you don't want to go backwards. So keep moving forward—even if it takes much longer than you'd hoped.*

And God would often sustain me through a friend passing along a healthy treat, an inspiring article, or an encouraging note in my mailbox. These became known as visitations from the Mail Box Fairy, or MBF. Taken all together, God and the Mail Box Fairy really kept me going in light of my all-too-shallow reservoir of motivation.

If you are one of the vast majority of women who wants to lose weight, I wish you the very best. It's not for the faint of heart. And it's not for those who expect to shrink to half their size in a matter of months.

Give it a year. Give it a *couple* of years. . . .

Habit is. . .
not to be flung out the window,
but to be coaxed down the
stairs one step at a time.[1]

MARK TWAIN

. . . .

If at first you don't succeed,
before you try again,
stop to figure out
what you did wrong.[2]

LEO ROSTEN

. . . .

I've been on a diet for two weeks,
and all I've lost is two weeks.[3]

TOTIE FIELDS

Reflections on Your Well-Lived Laugh—
Designing a Life That Keeps You Smiling

1) On a scale of 1 (being lowest) to 10 (the highest), how much does the pressure to lose weight bother you?

2) What are two or three words that describe how you feel about this pressure now?

3) What are two or three words that describe how you would feel if this pressure were lessened or removed?

4) Looking at your answers 1–3, on a scale of 1 to 10, how motivated are you to reduce this pressure?

5) Who is someone with whom you feel emotionally safe—who will encourage you while you decide how best to reduce this pressure?

6) Use this space to write some thoughts or feelings that this pressure has brought to your mind.

7) If this pressure negatively impacts your life in a significant way, try finishing this sentence:
I want to live well, laugh often, and smile more! I can begin by choosing to take this one step. . .

2
Serendipity at Risk

The Pressure to Be Intentional

Intentionality has been a big buzz word among Christians in recent years. On the heels of the blockbuster book *The Purpose Driven Life* have come others like *Your Best Life Now* and *One Month to Live,* all sounding the seize-your-days alarm. The authors, wise guys of the best kind, remind us that a life is a terrible thing to waste. As such, ordering our steps in the direction we want our lives to go is an admirable endeavor *if* we're careful to let God be our trail blazer.

For some of us, though, the pursuit of purpose has morphed into hypervigilance. Before we know it, even God Himself can't elbow His way onto our calendars. And we're exhausted from the constancy of all the disciplines and activities we're juggling to make our lives ultra-meaningful. We sense that something's missing, but *what* exactly? Well, it could be that we forgot how to leave room for serendipity: *discovering desirable things unexpectedly.*

Surprised by Serendipity

I recently ran across an essay I'd written years earlier; it reminded me just how powerful it can be to discover valuable things unexpectedly. Whether you thrive on schedules and routine or prefer lots of white space on your calendar, I hope you'll find some inspiration from my trip down serendipity lane seven years ago. It was a time before the economy went south (and decided to take up residence there). My husband, Scott, was blessed with well-paying, interesting work in television marketing. This allowed me to be a full-time homemaker when my children were small—a lifestyle I cherished.

They're Only Young Once

I thoroughly enjoy my children; more often than not, finding them to be adorable, funny, and fascinating. These are the children who, when given tempera paint, will create Cirque Du Soleil faces on each other if afforded half a chance via a parent's turned back. The same children will fight with teary-eyed fury over ownership of the family's self-inflating whoopee cushion. It's a dream come true for every hyperventilating parent who's been faced with the fiftieth plea of "Blow it up again!"

Though in this season of raising two pre-schoolers, my hand would be the first to shoot up if a researcher surveyed my mommy group with the question, "Who feels overwhelmed and on the cusp of insanity?" That said, having seen my son grow from a chubby-fisted toddler barely able to hold a basketball to a muscular ball boy for the Dallas Mavericks, I possessed a heightened awareness that the weeness of my two little girls would be for a short time. As such, I resolved to squeeze all the good out of these fleeting years as was womanly possible. And it's against this backdrop of my motherly resolution, that the following circumstances evolved:

I'm a Nut in a Rut, Amen. . .

A while back, our young family was hitting a wall. After living seventeen years on the East Coast in close proximity to the Atlantic Ocean, Colonial Williamsburg, and the Blue Ridge Mountains, we now found ourselves in Texas sub-suburbia with great schools and nice neighbors, but not a lot to do unless you like to fish for crawdads.

Not to rain on anyone's semismall town parade, but tying a raw chicken heart on a string and tossing it into a muddy creek isn't exactly my idea of a thrilling afternoon. Unless perhaps there's a coffee kiosk within walking distance of the bait shack; then I'm all over that—give me a caramel macchiato in one hand, raw chicken heart in the other, and I'll be the happiest woman in waders down at the crick shouting, "Polly put the kettle on—we're having crahfish for dinnah!" Sometimes all it takes is a spoonful of espresso to help a city girl get the pseudo-country life down.

But lately I've been longing for. . .more.

So here we were forty minutes from civilization and culture, and when faced with strapping our young and restless into car seats as the world turned ugly inside the van for the other passengers, we rarely ventured out, and thus became "town bound." After three years as residents in our new community, our greatest social achievement was that we were on a first-name basis with the Walmart cashiers.

Add to that my husband's hour-plus commute through downtown Dallas traffic that decreased our family time and increased his blood pressure, and we were slowly but steadily becoming a stuck-in-a-rut, disconnected, stressed-out family. What's worse (as a creative person, it pains me to pen this) our family was becoming *boring*.

One day as I was contemplating our plain vanilla plight, I told Scott, "I have an idea." My husband says he could make a life-size replica of Noah's ark if he had a wooden nickel carved from gopher bark for every time I uttered this loaded phrase. But because he, too, is partly creative by nature and possesses a fun-fueled pilot light buried deep within his otherwise highly structured persona, Scotty has learned to lend me an ear—even if some ideas crawl right on through his brain and exit out the other ear, like earwigs in a horror movie.

Anyway, on to the idea at hand. . .

I suggested to Scott that we conduct an experiment to help revive our waning sense of fun and adventure. The remedy? Take out a three-month lease on an apartment near exciting venues in downtown Dallas, which would put us halfway between our sub-suburban home and my husband's job. "It would be an urban getaway," I coaxed. Then, employing my most-ardent persuasion skills, I added, "Our little cabin in the city." We calculated the cost to be roughly what we would spend on a weeklong Florida vacation once we added up airfare, theme park admissions, and lodging. But this way, we would have three months of mini-vacations.

So we began making regular escapes to Big D—or *Dowass*, as my girls called it. Since the girls were in preschool just two days a week, the three of us spent several midweek overnight stays as well.

The World Is Our Oyster (and the Backyard Is Popcorn Shrimp)

One gloriously sunny, unseasonably warm winter day, the girls and I awoke at the Special Hotel, as we affectionately nicknamed the apartment. After good-morning kisses, I headed to the kitchen to whisk some eggs for my chicks. The girls were nested into their child-sized seats at the play table in front of the sliding glass door—happily coloring in their Cinderella coloring books.

My diminutive artiste, Tori, looks every bit like a miniature Audrey Hepburn—her soulful brown eyes, delicate cheekbones, and upturned nose framed by wispy brunette bobbed hair. Little sister Whitney, with her sandy-brown hair and almond-shaped eyes, possesses all the cuteness of Meg Ryan wrapped in the expressiveness of wide-eyed Buckwheat of Little Rascals fame.

"Hey!" I began, in an unseasonably warm voice. (A sunny day and a change of venue does wonders for this mom on the edge.) "Where would you girls like to go today?"

I poured the lemon-yellow mixture into the waiting skillet and wondered why my upbeat request was met with silence. I momentarily turned my attention away from the scrambling eggs to glance at the girls. I couldn't help but grin. They had pulled their chairs away from the table and placed them facing the wide sliding glass door, theater-style. The girls were clearly enthralled by their newfound bird's-eye view of a cleared lot, two stories below.

I turned the burner down and moved to the living room for a closer look at what was holding them in rapt attention.

What I saw were about fifty, hard-hatted Bob the Builder types working with the industrious effort of an ant colony: cement trucks were pouring out their contents like a huge mixer dispensing cake batter; cranes and bulldozers lifted steel beams and enormous rocks as if they weighed no more than chocolate bars and marshmallows. To my girls it must have seemed as tif hey'd stumbled upon Willy Wonka's Rocky Road Factory.

I will grant you, that from a preschooler's perspective, the rumbling scene below possessed a certain appeal. But hey, we didn't get this apartment in Trendy Town just to go south, culturally speaking. As I headed back to the kitchen, I thought, *The St. John-Gilberts are no run-of-the-mill country bumpkins easily sidetracked by the eye candy of a common construction site. No! We are avant-garde thrill seekers, ready to take Big D by double stroller!*

"Girrrls!" I called again, raising my voice to make sure they heard me this time. "Mommy was asking where you would like to *go* today—there's the art museum, the children's museum, Peter Rabbit's Garden at the arboretum, the Jungle Book play land at the Galleria mall, or. . ."

It was no use. No matter how lively my commercial, the day's offerings might as well have been on mute. Just when I thought I had rescued my offspring from the clutches of creativity-stifling sub-suburbia, I found myself upstaged by workmen in red flannel shirts toting mailbox-shaped lunch boxes.

As I placed an Elmo plate now filled with eggs and bacon in front of Tori, she asked excitedly, "Mom, did you see *that*?"

"What, sweetie?" I replied, forcing a fake smile.

"That ball thingy!" she exclaimed, her tiny body a-shiver with excitement. "Watch it. It's gonna crash into that wall and smash it to pieces—watch!"

"Neat, honey," I answered, digging deep for sincere validation of her wonderment. "Let's talk later about some fun places we can *go* today, okay?"

"Sure, Mom," she answered, her eyes locked on the scene before her as if it were the Macy's Thanksgiving Day Parade.

Well, I thought, with a feeling of resignation, *if you can't beat 'em, join 'em.*

Since we were obviously going to be spending a leisurely morning in, I looked around the apartment for something that would keep *me* entertained until my girls finished watching the live show from down below. And suddenly, like an oasis appearing on the horizon, there it was. . .

A bathtub. . .and bubbles.

Flexible R Me

Ah, the luxury of a leisurely bath while both girls were in the vicinity and not interrupting me—it was not only surreal; it was hugely therapeutic. While my skin was pickling nicely in the hot, sudsy water, Tori and Whitney moved seamlessly from watching Boom Town below, to playing with the sparse toy supply we had brought from the house—a handful of Barbies sans accessories, a few kiddy cooking utensils, and crayons and paper. "After all," I had told my husband before implementing the apartment plan, "the girls and I will be busy out on the town expanding our horizons—we won't need a lot of toys." As I continued basking in the warm bubbles with the girls out of my fragrantly shampooed hair, I thought, *Maybe the Amish are on to something—give the kids a few simple toys, no television, and—voilà—instant contentment.*

A couple of hours passed, and I, now neatly dressed, perfectly coiffed, and appropriately

makeupped, declared, "It's time to go bye-bye!"
By then, the call of hunger was on us all—so it
was an easy sell.

Even so, I had tasted the bounty of letting
the day unfold, having bagged some rare,
invigorating "alone time." And I was looking
forward to more of the same in our Dowass
getaway.

· · · · · · · · · · · · · · Unplugged · · · · · · · · · · · · · · ·

If it's been way too long since you've made room in your
life for serendipity, it's not too late to start. Though if
you're a techie, you'll need to unplug (at least a little) in
order to keep from being pulled back into the details of
your carefully devised master plan. Or someone else's.

Admittedly, unplugging is easier for me because I'm
not a techie. If you could be a fly on our walls, you'd see
through those thousands of microscopic lenses of yours,
that we do not have a television. Well, actually we do
have a television, but we don't receive any TV *stations*.
We watch movies on our DVD player or classic TV
shows like *McHale's Navy* on Hulu.

I'm also the world's slowest texter—my vocabulary

in this medium is a dozen words, few of which bear much resemblance to the actual words they represent: U no? I did try Facebook very briefly (and that, only under an assumed name), interacting with exactly three friends in Virginia with whom it's harder for me to stay in touch. After a year, we all stopped Facebooking each other. The novelty had worn off and we concluded that there was an addictive aspect to the whole shebang that infringed on our already limited time. Much to my sister's chagrin, as close as we are, I refuse to friend her for fear I'll get hundreds of friend requests from mutual acquaintances. Becky is so well connected and beloved, it's like having Elvis for a sibling. The prospect of making endless Facebook friends, for me, would be similar to getting caught in a crocodile death roll—once I got rolling, there would be no stopping.

Anyway, the point remains: The more distractions you have, the less likely you are to experience serendipity—someone, somewhere will want your time and attention. As it turns out, *time* and *attention* are two vital ingredients needed to discover desirable things in unexpected ways. I know this seems extravagant in our current "make every minute count" environment. . .but making room for unscheduled time in your life is the first step toward experiencing serendipitous moments.

Then we only need to pay attention.

It's often in the quiet, unrushed hours of our days that our hearts become receptive to valuable things— like contemplating song lyrics that express how we feel about something important to us; feeling how velvety soft and surprisingly comforting a puppy's tongue is on our hand; reconnecting with an old friend who just walked into the coffee shop; writing a note and including an encouraging scripture to someone who needs a lift.

Now if you're a hard-core planner by nature, even with all my schmaltzy prose, you may be thinking, *Serendipity, schmerendipity.* Well, in your case, perhaps a little will go a long way. And, to be fair to the more structured set, it's worth pointing out that some of us free spirits can benefit from a little more intentionality.

Regardless of where you land on the serendipity continuum, an old adage rings true for everyone. . . eventually: "Life is what happens to you while you're busy making other plans." So, at the very least, learning to accentuate the positive in the unexpected can be a vital coping skill when we're faced with circumstances that don't fit neatly into our preconceived grid.

It's often the detours of our lives that impact us the most—causing us to change our destinations. Sometimes the uncharted paths we suddenly find ourselves traversing turn out to be A-OK—we realize that if had stayed the original course, we would have missed out on something much better. But other more treacherous territory can leave us feeling like we're floating in a black hole, flailing about in complete darkness. We may attempt to remain optimistic, thinking, *Maybe God will send me a shiny silver jet pack soon.* But if time lurches slowly onward, our optimism is likely to fade into realism. We begin to think, *Boy, what I'd give for a Cracker Jack compass right now.*

Even when our best-laid plans have been interrupted by unforeseen circumstances, every day holds the promise of one phenomenal experience: having the comfort and counsel of the Holy Spirit as we head into our yet-to-be-lived hours. The longer I live, the more precious those hours become. My tolerance for "marking time" is getting lower by the decade. In that way, I guess this less-structured woman could be the poster girl for the Intentional Lifestyle.

But "seizing my days" has become less about my

well-thought-out plans and more about holding my days with an open hand before God. I want, above all, to discover the valuable things *He* wants me to see— whether through intentionality or. . .serendipity.

Serendipity. Look for something,
find something else,
and realize that what you've found
is more suited to your needs
than what you thought you
were looking for.[1]

LAWRENCE BLOCK

. . . .

You don't reach Serendipity
by plotting a course for it.
You have to set out in good faith for
elsewhere and lose your bearings.[2]

JOHN BARTH
The Last Voyage of Somebody the Sailor

Reflections on Your Well-Lived Laugh—
Designing a Life That Keeps You Smiling

1) On a scale of 1 (being lowest) to 10 (the highest), how much does the pressure to be intentional bother you?

2) What are two or three words that describe how you feel about this pressure now?

3) What are two or three words that describe how you would feel if this pressure were lessened or removed?

4) Looking at your answers 1–3, on a scale of 1 to 10, how motivated are you to reduce this pressure?

5) Who is someone with whom you feel emotionally safe—who will encourage you while you decide how best to reduce this pressure?

6) Use this space to write some thoughts or feelings that this pressure has brought to your mind.

7) If this pressure negatively impacts your life in a significant way, try finishing this sentence:
I want to live well, laugh often, and smile more! I can begin by choosing to take this one step. . .

3
Forty Something and Counting. . .Obsessively

❖

The Pressure to Stay Young

Several years ago, a friend of mine found herself with blurred vision at age fifty-plus. *Seems kind of early for this sort of thing,* she thought, and trotted off to see her optometrist. After eyeing her carefully, the optometrist suggested she see a really good ophthalmologist. The diagnosis? Detached retina.

After surgery, my friend was consigned to live for two weeks in a contraption that kept her lying face-down, surveying the landscape of her living room carpet. With so much thinking time, my normally sunshiny friend occasionally turned pensive. When the experience was over, she shared two of her many discoveries: "My carpet needs cleaning," she deadpanned, "and every ten-year mark brings significant changes to my body."

I am totally there right now. Having turned forty-seven this year, it feels like I've hit fifty already. I was okay with forty-six, but somehow forty-*seven* crossed a line in my psyche that had me obsessively ruminating about the changes occurring in my face and physique. At first, I was in denial. I would look at recent photos of myself or study my visage in the mirror and think, *Ah. . .come on now. It's not so bad. You still look. . .maybe. . .forty-two. . .ish.*

But the other day, as I stared intensely into my magnified makeup mirror, I realized I really don't look a day over—or under—forty-seven. So I'm working on coming to grips with the fact that I look just "shy of fifty." Along the way, I've noticed that my younger friends have grown weary of my midlife yammering.

"Stop the whining already," they demand. And the bolder ones will say, "You're not fifty. . .yet." I can't tell if they're trying to make me or themselves feel better by postponing a discussion of the inevitable. Because—mark my word—their "shy of fifty" day will come. Like the grim reaper. Sissies.

Time Travel

I can't fault the young and beautiful in my Rat Pack, because they're right. I am constantly noticing the women ahead of me in time travel by ten years or so. I actually annoy myself with my new addiction to scrutinizing the aging process. In my mind's eye, I often squint and try to make out how I might look with *more*: more wrinkles, more pounds, more age spots. Taking copious mental notes on "dos and don'ts," I highlight in fluorescent yellow the indispensable concealing tips: knee-length skirts, capri pants, tunic-style shirts, turtleneck sweaters, hair highlights, and (for those who can afford it and have a sturdy pain threshold), a buffet of cosmetic procedures.

Camouflaging strategies aside, it has puzzled me how some mature ladies get to look like Meryl Streep as they age while others. . .not so much. Just a shot in the dark, but I'm guessing most Meryls work hard at it—and Meryl admirers-from-afar, not so hard. I was surprised to learn that the over-forty women I know who look like movie stars actually do work out a lot. Who knew? They also eat about 1,000 calories a day—give or take a couple hundred. Yep, you read that right—per day—not per meal.

As to exercise, given the accompanying nightly body aches, I'm on the fence with the intensity and amount I'm willing to do at this late juncture. Most mornings I'll say to myself, "I think I'll jog with the dog today." But once I get out the door and start noticing things like the adorable finch with a brown crew cut, a dewdrop sliding down a blade of grass, a tuxedo-coated cat rubbing his back on our sidewalk (this is the occupational hazard of a writer)—thirty minutes later I'm back at my front door thinking, *I'll just write about jogging today.*

It's not just the physical changes that get under my loosening skin. There's also the realization that, statistically, I've lived more than half my life. *Half my life,* for crying out loud! This fact alone lends itself both to crying out loud and to intensive introspection.

One line of thinking flitting about my brain goes something like this: This stage of life is not that different from the awkward teen years—you're no longer a kid, but you're not a grown-up either. In this case, you're no longer a spring chicken, but your turkey neck has yet to arrive.

I finally decided it was time to push past these maddening poultry analogies and speak with Mother Goose, I mean, Mom. Maybe she could help me make sense of the awkward stage I found myself in.

"Surely there are hard-won benefits that balance the unsettling aspects of getting older," I implored, my hound dog eyes staring a hole into hers. My mother, who is in her midseventies, didn't seem all that concerned about her own aging. She was benevolent enough to ease my angst by delineating some of the perks.

"If it weren't for the aches and pains, I'd say this is probably the happiest time of my life," she said. "I like to think that after a lot of living, I've become wiser. At least wiser in caring less what people think of me and seeking more of who God wants me to be. Most women my age have pretty much settled the issues of who's the best looking, who has the most money, whose kids are the most popular, successful, smart, and so on. The jockeying for status finally subsides, and it's a great relief.

"Not to worry, honey. There are benefits to limping over the hill with a cane," she added, "though, it's true, they are more internal than external."

I was heartened to hear Mom's perspective. But some days I'd be willing to remain an insecure middle schooler inside if I could erase some of the wear and tear outside. At this very moment, assessing the spider veins on my legs, I'm thinking, *I wonder if it might be cheaper to tattoo over these than have them erased by a laser?*

Let's see—how many letters are there in "Born to Be Mild"? If I ask an exceptionally gifted tattoo artist to use two-inch-tall lettering, it will just about cover what looks like the handiwork of a toddler left alone with a red pen and a white couch.

• • • • • • • • • • Face(lifting) the Facts • • • • • • • • • •

After months of contemplating aging, I've concluded that midlife is similar to being pregnant for the first time. At least, that's the last time I remember being so preoccupied with my changing body.

Pregnant with my first child, I couldn't wait to see

how I would look with a baby bump. I'd stare dreamily at other women who were further along in gestation, their middle poking out prominently, nicely filling in the Lycra band of their maternity jeans. *If only* my *belly would poke out,* I remember thinking. I would have loved having a security guard announcing my arrival every time I went to the grocery store, clearing a path with a bullhorn. "Belly coming through!" I'd imagine him announcing loudly, as all eyes turned to focus on my burgeoning bump.

How it pains me to write those words now.

Twenty years later, what I wouldn't give to trade my outie for an innie. Nowadays, I just trudge down the grocery aisles, stopping now and then to massage my thigh as my sciatica flares up on the way to the Activia yogurt section. Please tell me I'm not the only woman who silently hopes Jamie Lee Curtis's DNA is mixed in with the probiotics in every cup.

Those memories of early pregnancy and the race to "get a bigger belly" lead my thoughts all the way back to the obstetrician's office. Of course, getter bigger had a point in that case. I distinctly remember staring enviously at moms in the waiting room who had recently delivered their offspring. They would sit contentedly next to carriers sporting tiny creatures who were wrinkled and ruddy and looked like seven pounds of newborn hamster.

I would try to envision what my own baby would look like—but all I could conjure was the outline of a two-pound kidney bean that mysteriously appeared on my sonogram. (The doctor said this was a picture of my baby, but the sonograms of the 1990s left a lot to the imagination.) Eventually, the baby did come, and he had a face—a very distinct and adorable one. Much better than a legume. While Trevor was a keeper, there were some leftovers I wanted to return—namely, the fat deposits that remained in the belly I had relished for the previous nine months.

Twenty years later I'm still working to de-emphasize that particular section of my torso. My baby boy is now a senior in college—which keeps me well reminded that I'm no longer part of the young and restless. Honestly, I can do without the restless part. But the loss of young is tougher to swallow, leaving a lump in my throat from time to time.

If you're near my age (or a decade or two ahead), you know the score—the New You is now the Old You. So what to do? Well, we have options—from shape-shifter swimwear to age-defying cosmetics to color-treated coiffures. If you have means and the inclination, there are many techniques (some more invasive than others) designed to shore up those "special features" we prefer not to feature. If you don't have the means, inclination, or constitution to have work done, go the natural route. Personally I'm both economically challenged and a pain wimp, so you won't need to bring any post-op casseroles to my door. Unless it's for a herniated disk covered by Medicare.

Whatever you do, try to make peace with your changing look. Here's where developing a positive perspective can really help. You're likely to be more attractive if, like the children's song, "You're Happy and You Know It." According to the scriptures, *inner* beauty secrets like contentment and joy are always worth cultivating.

•••••• Something Old, Something New ••••••

Mulling over getting older brings the phrase "aging gracefully" to mind. I loved the look that actress Audrey Hepburn had late in her life—she wore flowing tunics in gauzy fabrics that made her look so casually elegant. Sure, she was a picture-perfect celebrity, but she knew how to work that natural look in a way that didn't intimidate the rest of us.

When our looks are taking it on the double chin, most of us will discover there is another benefit of advancing age: Life can offer new beginnings and deeply satisfying experiences that we never dreamed would be ours for the taking. That is, unless you're like me and gave birth to two children when you were shy of forty. In that case, life may still open up for you after your children graduate college, but you may need a walker to get through the portal.

For those of you now on the glorious cusp of an empty nest, you may be encouraged by women who have found exciting and fulfilling second careers or philanthropic endeavors later in life. One friend of mine found unexpected satisfaction in becoming a high school teacher, allowing her to reconnect with a love of literature. Another friend, a former interior designer, began leading Bible studies for women who were incarcerated—she loves watching God redesign the interiors of the downtrodden. And my daughter Whitney has become friends with a woman who operates a rescue called Throwaway Ponies. The nonprofit works with local law enforcement to help horses that have been abused or neglected.

There are other fascinating stories of women who

have made significant contributions at midlife and beyond. I hope, like them, all of us will work out our own unique perspective on growing older. It's not easy because, well, there's some humble pie to be tasted as we come to terms with the newer reality of our older facades. But a forward-moving perspective at this juncture is so important to a life well-lived. After all, if statistically you've lived about half your life, there's no time like the present to envision the years ahead—they are there for the shaping.

If nothing else, getting older doesn't last forever. It does eventually end, which is perhaps the epitome of good news/bad news. And of course my mind had to go there.

During my prolonged weight-loss campaign, my thoughts turned suddenly morbid upon hearing of the death of an acquaintance who had been about my age. I started to sweat the small stuff and wondered what would happen if *I* died before I met my goal weight. What if my circumference required the starting lineup of the Texas Rangers as pallbearers and a team of Clydesdales to move me from the chapel to my final resting place? Mercifully, I was able to calm these irrational thoughts, and eventually they even turned optimistic.

"Well," I decided, "there's always cremation."

Forty is the old age of youth;
fifty is the youth of old age.[1]

Victor Hugo/French Proverb

. . . .

You know you're getting old
when the candles cost more
than the cake.[2]

Bob Hope

Reflections on Your Well-Lived Laugh—
Designing a Life That Keeps You Smiling

1) On a scale of 1 (being lowest) to 10 (the highest), how much does the pressure to stay young bother you?

2) What are two or three words that describe how you feel about this pressure now?

3) What are two or three words that describe how you would feel if this pressure were lessened or removed?

4) Looking at your answers 1–3, on a scale of 1 to 10, how motivated are you to reduce this pressure?

5) Who is someone with whom you feel emotionally safe—who will encourage you while you decide how best to reduce this pressure?

6) Use this space to write some thoughts or feelings that this pressure has brought to your mind.

7) If this pressure negatively impacts your life in a significant way, try finishing this sentence:
I want to live well, laugh often, and smile more! I can begin by choosing to take this one step. . .

4

One Friend's Trash Is Another Friend's Treasure

The Pressure of Rejection

Some years ago, the makers of my favorite candy bar ran an ad campaign in which an unsuspecting person eating a chocolate bar collides with someone else eating spoonfuls of peanut butter out of a jar. At first the people are stunned and incensed. One accuses the other with, "Hey! You got chocolate on my peanut butter!" The other retorts, "You got peanut butter on my chocolate!" Then, in a flash of mutual ingenuity, they taste the resulting concoction, and the most addictive candy bar of all time is born. Suddenly, all is very right with their world, as is always the case whenever I eat a Reese's cup—or two, or three.

Would that all unforeseen collisions had such funny and appetizing outcomes. But if you're old enough to have lived, say, past kindergarten, you realize this is not the case. Collisions can cause serious damage. And in the case of friendship gone awry, colliding perspectives can cause emotional concussions—throwing a knock-out punch to self-esteem.

The Peanut Butter Cup Factor (When Perspectives Collide)

Recently, I was all set to tap away at the computer keyboard, doling out humorous and encouraging anecdotes about owning our own perspective. Relevant topic in sight, diet Dr Pepper on tap, I emerged from a writing sabbatical ready to mix it up again with unconventional readers.

Before diving into writing, as I opened my e-mail, my bubbling enthusiasm fizzled. I realized a good friend had just experienced a very unfunny relational collision with someone important to her. Leigh had been one of several stay-at-home moms in my circle of friends. Over the previous two years, Leigh had been thrust into the dual roles of breadwinner and single mother, courtesy of her husband's midlife crisis. Her message read:

> *Hi Rachel,*
>
> *I need a safe place to vent this morning, so here goes. . .*
>
> *I've had a good friend for several years. She has a crazy sense of humor, and we just clicked and could talk about anything—and we did.*
>
> *But, as you know, my divorce turned my world upside down. All along this friend seemed so supportive. Then she suddenly stopped answering my phone calls, texts, and e-mails. If I saw her at church or school, she'd smile nervously, avoid eye contact, and disappear. I finally got the nerve to apologize—that if I had offended her or made her uncomfortable, it was never my intention and I*

would feel awful about it.

She curtly thanked me for the apology and offered no explanation for her sudden withdrawal from my life. After some time passed, she finally admitted that she didn't know how to relate to me now that I was divorced. She couldn't handle the situation anymore. She couldn't handle me anymore.

I feel like a schoolgirl shunned by someone I had admired and looked forward to seeing. I am so hurt and confused.

My heart broke for Leigh—she fit most everyone who knew her like an old shoe. It was inconceivable to me that someone could not see the treasure she was and offer her grace when she needed it most. I quickly wrote back:

Oh Leigh,

I wish I could give you a big hug right now and tell you in person, "This is her loss!" This may be as much (or more) about her as it is you. So try not to be too hard on yourself, okay?

It might help a little to know that psychologists who have researched rejection believe it to be one of the most painful emotions we experience. It can trigger the pain

center of your brain, causing that stomach-in-knots
feeling and can take a long time to heal.

In the meantime, know that God loves you. I love
you. And a whole bunch of other people do, too!

P.S. Would you like me to go beat her up or toilet
paper her house? 'Cause you know I would totally do that
for you.

I had barely bound up the wounds of my friend's
shredded heart when I was blindsided by a relational
collision of my own—one that managed to put a dent
in my appetite for a few days. (Which is really saying
something for a gal who can put away three Reese's
peanut butter cups if given an empty house and no
witnesses save the dogs. Luckily, they don't fink on me as
long as I bribe them with chewies.)

Given the title of this book, it's probably no shocker
that I skew toward the artsy side of personalities. As
a writer, my nature is to contemplate the depth and
breadth of just about everything—from my navel to
why Einstein could develop the theory of relativity but
couldn't master the comb. So my tendency is to dive
deep into conversations and ask a lot of questions. Every
now and then, in hopes of deepening a relationship
that seems promising, I'll share something vulnerable

or try out some offbeat humor—in addition to brevity, Somerset Maugham observed that *impropriety* can be the soul of wit. But I realize that can be risky, especially with someone I don't know well, as it could boomerang back to me like a machete to the heart.

You can probably guess where this is heading.

Yep, I completely misread the endearing personality of a new acquaintance to be a mirror image of my own—desiring the same kind of relating that I desired. My deep sharing and unconventional wit swung back and cut me to the quick. This person, while charming and chatty, informed me that she was intensely private and found me to be—how shall I put this delicately?—overwhelming, invasive, and obnoxious. (I'm paraphrasing, but this is very close to the original Greek.) Her revelation caught me off-guard, because one of the greatest joys of my life is having connected conversations with friends. My close friends are the same way—they are connecty gals by nature.

Looking back, I felt a lot like I did when I was about ten years old and met a new friend ("Oh boy! We are sooo alike. We'll be best pals in no time!"). All I lacked was a Girl Scout uniform, braces, and braids— and a lick of good sense. I've since learned that the neurotransmitter oxytocin (also known as the "bonding hormone") is responsible for that giddy feeling that can come over women when we gather to powwow or play. The oxytocin boost one gets from a healthy friendship is actually a major stress reducer and is currently a hot topic of psychological research.

But this time, it was my turn to be reminded that women don't always seek the same thing in friendship— and I only had myself to blame. I hate to admit that I committed this novice error in good judgment. But you know what? I'm doing it because I've discovered that friendship rejection is a dirty little secret we women carry silently—precisely because it's so darn humiliating and painful. So there. My secret's out. I jumped the gun in a new relationship and blew my self-esteem to smithereens—for a couple of weeks. Maybe longer. Maybe I'm still in therapy. Heck, I'm not *that* open. I'll just keep you guessing.

Maybe you know the feeling? You meet someone who seems like she would make a terrific friend. You have a few lunches, share some victories, struggles, laughs. Maybe you send some funny (well, *you* thought they were funny) messages via various technologies punctuated with lots of smiley faces and LOLs. And just about the time you are feeling all Mr. Rogers-y and reaching for your cardigan as you prepare to croon "Won't You Be My Neighbor?," you realize your neighbor is cowering behind the fence, avoiding you and your precious LOLs and smiley faces at all costs. You realize, in fact, that today will not be a "beautiful day in the neighborhood" for you. It will instead be a very dark day somewhere in the slum of your pulverized heart.

So, how do we, as Cher says in *Moonstruck* as she slaps Nicholas Cage across the face, "Snap out of it!"? Well, it helps a little to realize there really is something called "wisdom born of pain." I should know. It's where I get most of my wisdom. I so wish there was a way to pick this stuff up secondhand. But no such luck.

What can we learn from these experiences so that we rebound from them more quickly if, God forbid, there *is* a next time? We can learn two things for sure:

Thing 1: One Woman's Trash Is Another Woman's Treasure

I learned at a deeper level what I had known to a lesser degree: Not every woman values the same things in relationships. And that's okay. Missing the mark with a desired friendship hurts like the numbing shot before a wound is stitched. But it's okay—most, if not all, of us make this mistake at least once in our lives.

After my latest woodshed visit, I've come to believe that life is too hard and too short to invest precious time in unfulfilling relationships. As one friend told me, "We should go where we are celebrated, not where we are tolerated." I think that's good advice for developing friendships unless God is clearly leading you to stay. But even then, the other person is free to make a different choice and move on.

As a rule, if you can be yourself completely with one friend and not with another, *Choose the one who is openly inspired by your God-given gifts and personality.* This is in large part how we experience "God with skin on"— we feel His love and often hear His voice through our close relationships. Now, if no such people exist in your life and you haven't a clue as to why, you might want to look into that with a counselor or mentor.

Thing 2: We Are Rock Stars to a Very Limited Number of People in Our Lifetimes

This means there is a much larger number who will never know or care that we even existed. But the more distressing number are those who will get to know us for a while and, when offered the once-in-a-lifetime opportunity to join our band's groupies, will say, "No thanks." Ironically, this cuts both ways: At some point *we're* the ones who choose not to accept friendship overtures offered to *us*.

But when you've been cut off from someone you really cared about, it can hurt like slamming your fingers in a car door every day for about a week or two. This is true unless you intentionally develop "rejection kryptonite" (skills to keep your self-esteem from plummeting) or you're a contented hermit. Then, maybe, the duration of your pain will be much shorter. Regardless, may that pain remind us to be extra gracious the next time *we* step back from an offer of friendship.

As you might suspect from that finger-in-the-car-door analogy, I've had more angst over friendship rejection than I care to admit. In fact, what finally began to take the edge off my pain was rereading a well-worn Philip Yancey book, *The Jesus I Never Knew*. It helped a lot to realize that even Jesus didn't get to be liked by everyone—even most everyone.

Yes, Jesus had His loyal groupies, and boy did He love them. This despite the fact that they were often clueless as to what He was all about. I can relate. I can almost hear Him sighing in Yiddish, "Oy-vey, after all we've been through? You still don't understand

Me?" But amazingly, Jesus seemed to love His closest companions as if they were somehow irresistible. He found comfort and joy in their company and even gave them nicknames. For all the trouble relationships can cause, apparently being alone is much worse—even for the Son of God.

Then there were the Pharisees who hung around the fringes of the crowds—sometimes thinking Jesus was intriguing, at other times believing He was too unconventional for comfort. The Sadducees just thought He was a dangerous nutcase. Let's just say that yours truly has "shared in the sufferings of Christ" on that score more than once. I suspect we all do from time to time. Who hasn't thought, "Am *I* crazy, or are *they*?"

Rejection is no cakewalk. It's more like taking your heart out for a leisurely stroll on a bed of hot coals. And even the Savior of the world wasn't immune to its sting.

• • • • • • The Funny Thing about Rejection • • • • • •

In the final analysis, it helps to realize that every woman is walking her own private life journey. Sometimes what *feels* like rejection is not really rejection at all. It may just be a collision of perspective—what one woman treasures, another woman tosses away as not her thing. And sometimes what feels like rejection is just bad timing. There may be logistical constraints, stressful circumstances, or a disparity in relational development that keeps a friendship from being the right fit at the right time.

All I know is, with God's help, I hope to have much less self-loathing the next time a relationship looks like a keeper but turns out to be a catch-and-release. Now, if I don't get this right, be on the lookout for my next blockbuster hit, straight from Serenity Lodge, titled *Laugh Yourself to the Psychiatric Ward.*

Seven years would be insufficient to make some people acquainted with each other, and seven days are more than enough for others.[1]

JANE AUSTEN

. . . .

Perfect friendship is rarely achieved, but at its height it is an ecstasy.[2]

STEPHEN E. AMBROSE
COMRADES

Reflections on Your Well-Lived Laugh—
Designing a Life That Keeps You Smiling

1) On a scale of 1 (being lowest) to 10 (the highest), how much does the pressure of rejection bother you?

2) What are two or three words that describe how you feel about this pressure now?

3) What are two or three words that describe how you would feel if this pressure were lessened or removed?

4) Looking at your answers 1–3, on a scale of 1 to 10, how motivated are you to reduce this pressure?

5) Who is someone with whom you feel emotionally safe—who will encourage you while you decide how best to reduce this pressure?

6) Use this space to write some thoughts or feelings that this pressure has brought to your mind.

7) If this pressure negatively impacts your life in a significant way, try finishing this sentence:
I want to live well, laugh often, and smile more! I can begin by choosing to take this one step. . .

5

The Siren Song
of Celery

❧

The Pressure to Eat Healthy

While most of us are familiar with the double-tailed mermaid that adorns every delicious cup of Starbucks coffee we consume, we may be less familiar with the mythology that accompanies this creature, known as a siren. It seems that she possessed such an alluring voice that weary, homesick seamen would become entranced at the sound of her serenading and steer their ship toward the lovely being. Where did this land them? Shipwrecked on a craggy shore. Doomed. Thus the phrase "siren song" has come to describe things that appear alluring at first but in the end lead one into ruin.

Take celery, for example. The one food you'd think harmless above almost any other we might name can actually kill you. Some years back, I read about a man who, after happily consuming a healthy lunch of tuna salad with chopped celery, went out to mow his lawn. Before he knew what hit him, he stopped breathing. His wife rushed him to the nearest hospital, where he was quickly diagnosed as being in anaphylactic shock.

Admittedly, this is an extreme example involving a food allergy. But it had me thinking, *With all the hype surrounding healthy food, is it really the panacea to all that ails us?* And then I ran across this article from Dr. Ben Kim titled "Orthorexia Nervosa: The Health Food Eating Disorder." One point really got me thinking:

Like all other solutions to difficult problems—dietary medicine dwells in a grey zone of unclarity and imperfection. It's neither a simple, ideal treatment, as some of its proponents believe, nor the complete waste of time conventional medicine has too long presumed it to be.[1]

I didn't know whether to stamp my feet in frustration over the bushels of carrots I'd eaten over the past year or breathe a sigh of relief as I cozied up to a half-pint of Funky Monkey full-fat ice cream. As we've discussed, life is about choices—and in the case of diet being able to cure all of our physical woes, apparently the choices aren't always crystal clear. Don't get me wrong: I would never discourage anyone from healthy habits. But my goal here is to encourage women to think for themselves before religiously adhering to someone else's menu.

· · · · · · · · · · · Healthy Eating— · · · · · · · · · · ·
All the Rage or Just Enraging?

In the past ten years or so, for better or worse (probably some of each), there has been significant pressure on Americans to eat healthy foods. So unless you're sequestered in a convent or live in the boondocks (both are possible, though it would be unlikely this book would have found you in either locale), you are likely aware of the health benefits of including more fruits, vegetables, whole grains, and lean protein in your diet and nixing fat food—Freudian slip—I mean *fast* food and sweets. Actually "fat food" *is* on the nix list, too, though more appropriately termed "fatty foods," which seems a disproportionately disparaging term for culinary delights such as savory blue cheese dressing, sublimely real butter, and mouthwatering whipped cream, but I digress.

There's also a growing group of food lovers who are opting for a vegetarian or vegan diet. The latter required my niece, Rachel Praise, to purchase a large food processor and move a cot into her kitchen, because that's where she spent most of her time—preparing fresh foods for her family and cleaning mountains of pots and pans after each meal. Just the thought of being married to my kitchen and doing enough dishes to make a restaurateur wince had me swearing off this way of eating.

I wondered if there might actually be a mental health benefit from including in our diets, at least on occasion, certain foods. Moon Pies, Snickers bars, bacon burgers, and macaroni and cheese—at the very least they can bring to mind cherished memories, thus boosting those happy-making endorphins that lift our moods to the stratosphere, however temporarily. Perhaps even long enough to get us on the treadmill.

I'll always remember the giddy feeling I experienced at summer camp while waiting for the concession stand to open. I remember counting up my change to buy a Hershey's milk chocolate bar and an icy cold Coca-Cola—I can almost feel the memory of the prickly carbonation lighting up my throat as it burned refreshment throughout my entire body.

No matter which side of the healthy-eating pendulum you swing on, I think we can all agree that the plethora of diet books indicates one undeniable truth: A lot of people love food. Many people enjoy preparing and sharing favorite recipes with friends and family. For them, it's a quality of life issue—a frequent pleasure they're not willing to reserve only for special occasions.

· · · · · · · · · Family, Friends, and Food· · · · · · · ·

Famous cooks such as Julia Child and Paula Deen—two women who have inspired so many passionate cooks to seize the day within their own kitchens—know that there's a connection between food and relationships that's important to foster. Both Child and Dean make room for some indulgence of classics like butter and sugar. On that score, I found the following snippets from an interview with Julia Child to be fascinating and encouraging:

I've always liked Child's zest for life and her unpretentiousness. Rabidly opposed to the low-fat food trend, she loves butter, bacon, and beef, and she's an advocate for enjoying all other elements of the good life— albeit in small portions. And she has even been known to eat an occasional Whopper or Big Mac.

Q: Could you sum up your feelings about the low-fat food movement?

A: I don't go for that at all. In the American Institute of Wine & Food. . .our motto is: "Small helpings. No seconds. No snacking. A little bit of everything, and have a good time." If you can follow that, it keeps your weight and health in good form. Even if you're going to have some rich dessert, you can always just have a little spoonful to taste it and keep your spirits up. Then I don't think you have to go into that miserable, low-fat stuff. [2]

I like that concept: a little bit of everything and have

a good time. It speaks to the idea that there are soul-nurturing, relationship-deepening aspects to cooking together and sharing delicious food at mealtimes. It's a chance to retell memories, share new stories, and laugh with each other around the dinner table.

Our family will never forget the night my school-aged sister temporarily forgot her manners, most likely out of playful mischief. My father turned his head to coax our neurotic Pomeranian, Po-Po, over for a scrap of ham, and Becky reached over my Dad's glass to stab a spiced peach from a bowl on the other side of his iced tea. As she attempted to bring the slippery prize back to her plate, the peach slipped off the fork and made a splash, landing in Dad's tea, lightly misting his glasses. We all sat bug-eyed for a minute then collapsed into laughter.

Just as laughter smoothes the often rocky road of life (and has been proven to have healing properties), so can the delight of preparing and eating food together. Take restaurateur Martha Hawkins, for example. Born the tenth of twelve children in Montgomery, Alabama, she overcame poverty and mental illness—achievements due in no small part to her passion for sharing home cooking. Her story has been featured in media outlets such as the *New York Times*, *Southern Living*, and *O, The Oprah Magazine*. Listen to the hints of her nurturing soul as she describes the common lima bean in this excerpt from her book *Finding Martha's Place*:

> *The lima beans at Martha's Place are cooked with a whole lot of love. When you put them against your lips they feel plump, like you was smooching the back of your baby grandson's knee. If you close your eyes and let them, those lima beans will remind you of sitting at home with all the people you love.*[3]

I have some idea how Martha Hawkins feels.

I was born in 1964 and spent many happy days in the 1970s growing up in suburban Texas. My mom was the consummate 1950s mother who kept a neat house and an even neater beehive hairdo—and made wonderful family meals nightly. Some of my favorite dishes included juicy fried chicken encrusted with Kellogg's Corn Flakes and a lasagna roll made with Italian spiced meats, mozzarella cheese, and tomato sauce, rolled up into a Pillsbury crescent roll crust, then baked to golden perfection. Our family obligingly consumed greens—broccoli, green beans, or salad—while counting the moments until dessert and coffee were served. Did I mention this went on nightly? Two specialty desserts vied for first place in our hearts and mouths. The first was homemade apple dumplings with a flaky crust so buttery the memory of it almost brings me to happy tears. The other contender was Mom's chocolate pecan caramel bars, also made with a crust laden with butter. Be still my heart. You may be thinking, "With all the butter backed up in your arteries, you may just get your wish."

Cholesterol count aside, I'm just saying that I understand the connection between "nurturing relationships and food." There's a warm connection that occurs between people when they gather for delicious meals thoughtfully prepared. This very dynamic has recently become the topic of popular books. *Forbes* magazine blogger and psychologist Todd Essig writes of his captivation with an acclaimed new book on the topic of food and human connectedness, *An Everlasting Meal*. He writes that the concepts of "food, comfort, pleasure and the balance of a well-lived life" as woven together in this charming, insightful volume often infiltrate his thoughts.

· · · · · Healthy Eating: *The* Key or *One* Key? · · · · ·

I'm not advocating a "no holds barred" approach to every meal we eat—we could end up resembling the wrestlers for whom that phrase was coined. Instead, I want to point out that insisting everyone eat the same way seems a bit heavy-handed and unrealistic. After all, what we eat is just one component (surely an important one) of our overall health. But there are many other things that greatly impact our health: exercise, smoking, food additives (intentional or otherwise, including hormones, preservatives, and pesticides), alcohol, recreational drugs, stress, an optimistic or pessimistic outlook, spirituality, and genetics.

Take, for example, Betty Ford who died at age ninety-three. It's no secret that she spent a good number of her years abusing her body with alcohol. She was certainly under significant stress as the wife of a president. You would think if anyone would have cut her life short by such influences, it would have been Betty Ford—but she lived almost a century.

I've known more than one Oklahoma cattle rancher who ate plenty of beef alongside his daily oatmeal and lived far longer than others who were more health conscious. If you stop and think about it, you could probably name other friends or family members who ate a "deadly diet" by today's standards yet lived to a ripe old age.

I know this makes many people nervous. It makes me nervous to write it. It's tempting to think that these folks are statistically in the minority, but a landmark, eighty-year study on longevity discussed in the book *The Longevity Project* affirms that though diet and exercise matter, neither appear to be among the top factors for a long life. In fact, the research discovered that it is "responsible, goal-oriented citizens, well-integrated into their communities" who are most likely to live long, healthy, and happy lives.

One of the authors, researcher Howard Friedman, said, "Connecting with and helping others is more important than obsessing over one's diet, rigorous exercise program, or work load."[4]

I'm not trying to provide excuses for poor eating or overeating. I'm merely suggesting that we need to be careful about pointing to food as *the thing* that will lead to an overall healthy life. Sure, it can be one component—and for those who struggle with food addiction, it's a significant component. But I think you'll find that savvy dieticians and personal trainers agree that the recipe for achieving joy and contentment in a broken world with imperfect people includes much more than greens and grains. If you've ever watched the hit TV show *The Biggest Loser*, you have no doubt seen that once the weight starts coming off, the real battle begins—dealing with the psychological tentacles of addiction.

Even if we could perfectly control our diets, we still can't control the unknown. We can't control the future. Think of it—no one can stop the proverbial Mack truck that might run us down and send our body, healthy or un, straight to its Maker. I've known at least two women "health nuts" who ended up with terminal cancer—well before the age of fifty. So if a person were to choose a less-than-optimum diet and considered that a quality of life choice, maybe we should live and let live.

Sometimes, though, the choices of someone we love impact *our* quality of life—including the pain of watching them suffer from those bad choices. If you find yourself in that situation with a food lover, maybe you can strike a deal with him or her: "If you eat lean and green Monday through Friday, we'll share a Moon Pie on the porch swing on Saturday night." Of course, if your loved one is a bona fide food addict, the stakes are higher, and you may have to sweeten the deal with more than the promise of a weekly Moon Pie—with all their marshmallowy goodness, they do have their limits.

And me? Well, I'm making peace with the allure of food through my aforementioned "fraternal twin foods." This has allowed me to enjoy eating without the self-loathing that had accompanied my tendency to overeat and indulge in too many unhealthy foods. My family's well-being became a huge impetus for my mealtime metamorphosis—I wanted to be able to stay active with my girls.

Recently I could tell I had made some progress when I volunteered to chaperone a hike on a mile-long trail littered with rocks of every shape and size. There were more moments when I felt like a capable tightrope walker—and fewer moments when I felt like an old fogey needing the assistance of a Saint Bernard with a first-aid barrel attached to his collar. Fortunately, I had the foresight to purchase hiking boots with roll bar technology to steady the ol' ankles. (Apparently roll bars aren't just for SUVs anymore.) With any luck, the next outdoor-wear gadget will be a baseball cap with a mini A/C unit installed underneath the bill.

But, back to family life and food.

I'm happy that restaurants are offering more healthy alternatives, and yet I wouldn't want those offerings to be mandated, putting things like kid meals in jeopardy. The other night, my nineteen-year-old-son sidled up to me with his hands behind his back and a big grin on his face. "Close your eyes and open your hand," he said, a bit coyly. I obliged, and when I opened my eyes, there lay in my palm a small red dragon toy.

"Where'd you get it?" I asked with a chuckle.

"Happy Meal," he replied as he gleefully snatched back his treasure and raced upstairs, I assume to relive some supersized childhood memories. I smiled, thinking that his discovery had come at a very good time for a kid who'd recently had his heart broken by a girl.

This talk of mandating healthy foods has me recalling the days of Prohibition. So I'm thinking if junk food is outlawed, we could have a resurgence of speakeasies that cater to the foodie in all of us. I can see it now:

It's a cold, rainy night, and I, cloaked in a black trench coat, approach the side door of a centuries-old row house near downtown. I rap softly on the door, and a round face needing a shave appears behind the peep slot and grates, "Passwoid?" I glance around uneasily, making sure I haven't been followed and whisper the magic word into the slot: "Cupcake."

Once in, I'm seated at a white-clothed table where I'm served plump, juice-dripping prime rib, twice-baked potatoes, and eventually that for which I've really come. My nerves are tense now, eager for the final fix— flourless chocolate torte. On the stage, the band strikes up a tune and Harry Connick Jr. emerges to croon the lyrics from "The Candy Man":

Who can take a rainbow, wrap it in a sigh,
cover it in cream and make a strawberry lemon pie?
The Candy Man. . .the Candy Man can,
'cuz he mixes it with love and makes the world taste good.

The emphasis on right eating even has me rethinking my theology. The more I feel the addictive pull of foods such as cheesecake, brownies, yeast rolls, and mozzarella-laden pizza, the more I'm convinced the forbidden fruit in the Garden of Eden was a starchy carbohydrate. I personally suspect the glazed donut, which is still found in even the most obscure of Texas towns. Perhaps there's no more appropriate symbol of man's struggle with the dark side than red velvet cake; though there's a compelling case to be made for devil's food—the name's no contest, of course. Whew! I'm getting high just *writing* about this stuff. I gotta quit before I fall off the wagon straightaway.

There's nothing to debate here: If we eat too many calories, they have to go *somewhere*. Rhoda Morgenstern, Mary's best friend on *The Mary Tyler Moore Show*, put it this way, "I don't know why I eat chocolate—I should just rub it on my hips." What *is* up for debate is whether pressure and mandates or encouragement and choice are the best tactics to spread the well-intentioned message that what we eat can have a significant impact on our overall health.

Enough said? Then let's eat!

No matter what kind of diet you are on, you can usually eat as much of anything you don't like.[5]

WALTER SLEZAK

. . . .

My wife is a light eater; as soon as it's light, she starts eating.[6]

HENNY YOUNGMAN

Reflections on Your Well-Lived Laugh—
Designing a Life That Keeps You Smiling

1) On a scale of 1 (being lowest) to 10 (the highest), how much does the pressure to eat healthy bother you?

2) What are two or three words that describe how you feel about this pressure now?

3) What are two or three words that describe how you would feel if this pressure were lessened or removed?

4) Looking at your answers 1–3, on a scale of 1 to 10, how motivated are you to reduce this pressure?

5) Who is someone with whom you feel emotionally safe—who will encourage you while you decide how best to reduce this pressure?

6) Use this space to write some thoughts or feelings that this pressure has brought to your mind.

7) If this pressure negatively impacts your life in a significant way, try finishing this sentence:
I want to live well, laugh often, and smile more! I can begin by choosing to take this one step. . .

6

Foreign Exchange Student

❧

The Pressure of "It's All Good"

I don't know about you—but the sun seems to shine a little brighter, and my troubles feel a little lighter the moment I step into my favorite coffee shop. Yesterday the spiky-haired barista greeted me with a gusto-infused "Good morning!" that seemed to spring more from his heart than his sales training. Happy customers sat hidden behind newspapers, engrossed in computers, or deep in conversation—such a cozy retreat from the bustle of daily life. Soon I would join them.

Aromatic elixir of joy in hand, I approached the condiment counter. With the cream pitcher poised over my steaming cup, I began to hum along with Louis Armstrong's version of "What a Wonderful World," lilting from the sound system. Then—somehow the pitcher slipped from my hand, toppling my precious coffee over neat piles of sugar envelopes, now resembling miniature sponges saturated with taupe-colored liquid.

"Oh no!" I whined. Heads popped up from newspapers and computers, conversations ceased, and an awkward silence filled the once-tranquil atmosphere. My mind's eye transported me back to the family dinner table when, as a schoolgirl, I spilled my milk. I could hear the collective gasp of my family and see them scooting back from the table, trying to avoid the oozing mess that was headed toward their laps.

I popped back to reality just in time to see that Mr. Smiley had leaped from his post at the espresso machine, coming with mop in hand to my aid.

"I'm so sorry," I blurted out with a sigh.

"No problem!" he insisted. "It's all good!" At that moment, I was reminded of Burt, the chimney sweep in *Mary Poppins*. With admirable efficiency, he swabbed up my mess, set a brand-new cup of joe on the counter, and pushed it toward me with a wink of approval. All that was missing was a choreographed rendition of "Chim Chim Cher-ee."

Throughout the shop, heads dipped back behind newspapers, fingers began clicking computer keys, and conversations recommenced. And me? I headed out the door with hope for a new day rising again in my spirit, self-esteem restored, and minimal self-loathing—thanks to a caring soul and that sunshiny phrase "It's all good."

It's a phrase that's used a lot these days, and I must admit, I like it. It's upbeat and forward moving—two things that truly help smooth over many of the rough patches of daily life. But I have to say, when it comes to the weightier issues of life, things are definitely not *all* good.

In fact, for the more contemplative among us, there is an ongoing inner struggle regarding things being painfully *not* "all good" here on earth. We Christians know in our heads "this world is not our home," yet our hearts are bound to this place where we spend our days with the people we love. So, honestly, while "it's all good" is a nice one-liner, what sounds like pleasant theology can be a source of consternation.

· · · · · · ·There's No Place Like Home· · · · · · · ·

The idea of this world not being our home reminds me of when I was a teenager and a teacher asked if I'd consider being a foreign exchange student. As much as I loved all things ambience-y and quaint—the kind of thing one would find at every turn in Europe—the thought of leaving everything and everyone familiar caused my stomach to tie itself in knots. Sure, my friends and family and I had our relational warts, but we loved and enjoyed each other. Most of all, we knew how to keep the laughter going even if nothing else was particularly peachy.

The thought of leaving my daily support to take up residence halfway around the world was paralyzing to me. And so, like my Visa Card, I had never left home without it—at least not longer than a week for summer camp. And I thought poorly of the idea for everyone else. I wanted to tell those on-the-fence, potential horizon expanders roaming the hallways of Lamar High School, "This exchange student stuff is a bad idea!" Yes, I was a homebody, and I knew where I belonged.

My senior year, I actually befriended a few exchange students from Germany and Finland. Despite the heartiest of welcomes from the most loving Texans, they were homesick—and half a world away from the remedy. They wanted their own moms and dads and friends (warts and all), but all they got was a goofy American who tried to help them find the light side in spite of the heaviness they often felt. "Gee, Jurgen, just think," I'd console, "only eight more months of misery till you can go back to Momma's schnitzel and speaking in complex sentences." And on every occasion when I found myself hugging yet another homesick traveler, their tears drenching my button-down shirts, my mind kept repeating, *They should have known this was a bad idea!* Yes, Dorothy's sage words proved right again: "There's no place like home."

While thinking of those friends, visiting America from the old country, I was hit with another pang of nostalgia, this one from my early twenties. As I spied a list of new e-mails on my computer, my eyes fell on the last name Blair. It was from an old roommate of mine—Becky Blair. We had worked together at a graduate school in Virginia. I couldn't wait to see what she was up to these days.

Becky and her sister Robyn had been bridesmaids in my wedding. They were both accomplished vocalists—Robyn was more fun than a barrel of spider monkeys, as my mom likes to say, and sometimes she made extra money singing commercial jingles on the radio. Becky was well-known around campus as a singer-songwriter. She had a sweet way about her and an infectious laugh. She was contemplative and possessed old-soul wisdom—a mark of how dramatically Jesus had touched her life. No one who knew her would have suspected that as a younger woman she suffered from agoraphobia (the fear of getting out and about) in her hometown of Danville, Virginia.

Becky and I had lost touch after her marriage and move to the Chicago area, though I had occasionally kept in touch with Robyn. All I knew was that Becky had a young son and seemed very happy in her new life. So, with a smile on my face and anticipation in my heart, I opened the e-mail, ready to reconnect with my friend. I quickly realized, though, that the message was not from Becky, but her sister, now Robyn Blair-Mitchell. It read:

Dear Rachel,

*I need to tell you that Becky has gone home to be
with the Lord she loved so much. She was diagnosed with
cancer and four weeks later was welcomed into the arms
of Jesus.*

Becky loved you very much.

I'll be back in touch soon,
Robyn

I stared at my computer screen, hot tears softly tumbling down my cheeks. I reread the message several times to make sure I really understood it.

Becky has gone home to be with the Lord she loved so much.
That phrase especially pierced my heart. It was very hard to believe this could be true—not the part about her loving Jesus so much, but the part about her being with Him and not with us. Don't get me wrong—I'm all for loving God, but going home with Him is quite another matter.

It's not like God is some grandfather figure you can go visit just for the weekend, sipping lemonade and chewing the fat on the front porch. No, "going home" in this case meant a one-way ticket with no possibility of return. For a few pensive moments, it occurred to me that perhaps Becky was one of those rare believers who loved God so much that the intensity of her love had become the catalyst to the next life. I thought of Brent Curtis, coauthor of *The Sacred Romance*, and his mountaintop topple into the next life, and of Rich Mullins, the celebrated singer-songwriter ("Awesome God," "Sing Your Praise to the Lord") whose Jeep became his one-way ride *home* on a midwestern highway.

Becky was a rarity in that same vein—an all-out believer who loved God with an uncommon passion. She had experienced Him firsthand. He had delivered her from the paralyzing grip of fear that had made her world too small for too long. And those are the daring Christians—the ones like the angel Gabriel who powerfully illuminate the lives of all they touch. They are challenging to unbelievers and waffling believers because they are bold in sharing their redemption stories and desperately want others to know the love and power of the living God.

Pictures flooded my mind—pictures of Becky's shy smile, dark brown eyes, and waiflike figure moving lightly down the hall of the university where we worked together. The next thing I knew, my gaze fell upon my sleeping toddler, laid out at the foot of my bed, her mouth wide open. A shard of fear shot through me, sudden and unexpected. My mind and emotions were still stinging with the reality of death and of being separated from those I cherish. Before I could edit my thoughts, my mind raced on: *If loving God deeply means I risk receiving a one-way ticket to go home with Him, I don't want to be a Christian right now. I'd rather live a long life with the people I love and have a deathbed conversion in my old age.*

· · · · · · · Not Now—How about Later? · · · · · · ·

Robyn's words—*Gone home to be with the Lord she loved so much*—made me uneasy. It was much like that rock-in-my-gut feeling I had about becoming a foreign exchange student. "Going home to be with the Lord" *sounds* pleasant and otherworldly, similar to "studying abroad." I'm all for European ambience—give me window boxes bursting with red tulips and cobblestoned villages to roam, and I'm all in. But getting almost "homesick" for heaven? I couldn't relate.

I can get behind the idea of loving God *here*—on earth. But going to His house for a face-to-face chitchat makes me nervous. It reminds me of a question my childhood girlfriend asked during Sunday school when Mrs. Schmidt asked if everybody wanted to go to heaven. Kathy looked at me and said, "Today?"

I'm with Kathy. It's a great idea for another day. For one thing, I know some little kids in my house who would miss me with a vengeance—kind of the way I was feeling now, realizing I would never see Becky Blair again on this earth. How I wanted to hold her pixie face in my hands and look her straight in those chocolate-brown puppy eyes and ask her one last question.

"Hey, missy," I'd begin," maybe you won't get homesick for us now that you're in paradise, but we're going to miss *you* like crazy. Did you think of *that* when you left? You can't just go 'be with the Lord' now! You can do that later, like for a special treat on your hundredth birthday. Then we'll *all* come with party horns and confetti and send you off with a bang and a cupcake covered in sprinkles. But not now. It's too soon. This was a very bad idea."

But the cold truth was that Becky was not on a foreign exchange program for a year. She was not going to return to us with stories of mountain men wearing lederhosen and wielding beer steins while singing polka songs at the top of their lungs. No, she had accomplished the spiritual equivalent of joining the Foreign Legion. Becky Blair, jovial friend to many, passionate singer-songwriter, and joy-filled wife and mother, was gone for good.

As sad as I was, I couldn't begrudge Becky the pleasure of living in the presence of Jesus.

And so my heartache began to give way to twinges of envy for a friend who had become a spiritual foreign exchange student—now returned to her homeland—the place where she most belonged. Ironically, Becky now lives where all Christians will someday feel most at home. For all my bellyaching about being a foreign exchange student, it is in truth, my lifelong reality. I live in a "country" that is not really my home.

Amazingly, in the weeks and months that passed, "gone for good" had a poignant double meaning for Robyn and her family—witness her note to me three weeks after Becky went home:

Hi, Rachel!

It was so great to hear from you. Though our family is experiencing grief, we are, as the scriptures say, "not without hope." As you know, Becky was always comfortable in the presence of Jesus—that is a great comfort to us now.

Let's keep in touch,
Robyn

After reading that, I felt like such a spiritual light-weight. Though I had been praying fervently for God to somehow, some way, comfort Robyn and her family—I admit that I had not expected such a brave, encouraging response.

This one sentence in particular greatly affected me: *Becky was always comfortable in the presence of Jesus—that is a great comfort to us now.* I thought back to the feelings I had had contemplating the foreign exchange program—how painful it would be to live far, far away from my familiar peeps. *Maybe Becky was like me—maybe she was a homebody. And when her physical body let her down, she knew where she belonged.*

I felt peace replacing the initial fear and grief. As much as I hate pain—and I hate it so much I sign my epidural consent the same day my pregnancy test turns blue—I was comforted by Robyn's courageous optimism. I mean, hard times blindside us all. So the idea that God can take the edge off—even of something this hard—is, well, stunning in the Catherine Zeta-Jones way of beauty and the Lance Armstrong way of triumph. Simply stunning.

"Going home to be with the Lord she loved so much." *Hmmmm.* That kind of had a sweet ring to it now.

A Place Where It's All Good, All the Time

A few years after Becky's death, I met an elderly woman who had raised her mentally handicapped son to early adulthood until he died of natural causes. Even now, many years down the road, she misses him—yet she's also happy for him to be finally whole. "After all," she said smiling bravely, "there are worse things than death." I could see her eyes moistening at the memories.

I had always thought this might be true—that there were many things worse than death, particularly when you consider heaven as the alternative. But now, hearing confirmation coming from this mother, it gave validation to my hunch.

One last comforting thought: Bible scholars do not believe Christians are destined to sit around singing and rearranging their crowns lying at God's gigantic feet. The word on the theological street is that this same earth we now occupy will be fully restored to the way it was before darkness came on the scene to pervert just about everything in it. A perfect world? As one songwriter put it so well, "I can only imagine."

Think of it: a pristine world. Unmarred mountains,

oceans, and continents to explore with abandon. Un-marred human hearts, connecting and caring without any relational or cultural baggage to muck things up. And perhaps best of all, no more infomercials, computer viruses, or whiny toddlers in need of a nap to drive us to the brink of insanity.

Jesus said, "I am the light of the world." Indeed, in the Bible, John writes that in heaven there is no need for any outside source of light—no sun, no moon, no streetlights—for God himself will envelop us with a light emanating from within His own being:

> *He'll wipe every tear from their eyes. Death is gone for good—tears gone, crying gone, pain gone—all the first order of things gone. . . . The City doesn't need sun or moon for light. God's Glory is its light, the Lamb its lamp!*
> REVELATION 21:4, 23

This image is so comforting to me—the image of the light of God chasing away the darkness of this broken world in which we live. Thankfully, when our lives grow dim—when cancer strikes; when planes fly into buildings; when hurricanes, divorce, or financial ruin sweep away the life we once had—God gives us earthly glimpses of light in darkness. Kind doctors. Brave rescuers. Loyal friends. Clean water, food, and shelter given in Christ's name. All of these things—and more—provide fodder for developing a perspective of hope when we face the inevitable reality that things are not "all good" on this planet.

Even though we cling to this life and can't imagine leaving those we love behind, something inside us can't stop longing for the day when we no longer "see through a glass dimly"—surviving only on glimpses of light here and there. We can't help but look forward to the day when we will see clearly the face of Jesus and *everything* that is wrong is made right.

I can only imagine. . .what Becky now sees. But I'm pretty sure it's all good.

In the midst of winter,
I found there was within me
an invincible summer.[1]

ALBERT CAREB

. . . .

Look not mournfully into the
past, it comes not back again.
Wisely improve the present, it is thine.
Go forth to meet the shadowy
future without fear.[2]

HENRY WADSWORTH LONGFELLOW

Reflections on Your Well-Lived Laugh—
Designing a Life That Keeps You Smiling

1) On a scale of 1 (being lowest) to 10 (the highest), how much does the pressure of "it's all good" bother you?

2) What are two or three words that describe how you feel about this pressure now?

3) What are two or three words that describe how you would feel if this pressure were lessened or removed?

4) Looking at your answers 1–3, on a scale of 1 to 10, how motivated are you to reduce this pressure?

5) Who is someone with whom you feel emotionally safe—who will encourage you while you decide how best to reduce this pressure?

6) Use this space to write some thoughts or feelings that this pressure has brought to your mind.

7) If this pressure negatively impacts your life in a significant way, try finishing this sentence:
I want to live well, laugh often, and smile more! I can begin by choosing to take this one step. . .

7

Moving On

The Pressure of Change

It's said that brevity is the soul of wit, and in the case of some two-word sentences that pack a punch, the emphasis is on *soul*.

Take, for example, these shorties with a bite: I'm sorry. Go away. Jesus wept. Grandpa died. In a world filled with constant activity and noise, these dynamic duos have the power to take our breath away, if just for a moment. The two-word sentence that knocked the wind out of me recently? We moved.

Yes, one very hot August we said good-bye to our home of ten years and the memories good and bad that were made within its walls. As it turns out, ten years is a significant chunk of living. For me it included, among other things, the birth of a baby, writing two books, graduating a teenager, gaining weight, losing weight, and the ups and downs of married life with kids.

Like so many other families in this jalopy of an economy, our pay doesn't quite cover our checks, and something had to give. Mercifully, we were able to sell our home—and at closing, let out a sigh of relief, thinking we'd settle back on the cushion of our equity until a stronger income came along.

One thing surprised us, though. Apparently, in a down economy, rents go up, sometimes by hundreds of dollars, as more people found themselves in our situation. In our neighborhood, good properties were getting multiple applications and top-dollar offers from would-be renters. This shot most rentals out of our price range. We would make a list of available homes, but literally by the time we placed a call to inquire, they had already been leased.

Tired of being the bridesmaid and never the bride, we knew we had to employ a new strategy. Our home was to close in two weeks, and the long and short of it was we didn't have a place to live. We briefly considered filling an envelope with a thousand bucks in unmarked bills and leaving it discreetly at a neighborhood park for a landlord willing to make a deal—but since we were broke, we thought the better of that.

After a lot of prayer and a little fasting, we were poised to say good-bye to our town and hello to the suburban hinterlands. Then it happened. One afternoon as I sat listlessly at the computer, I pulled up Realtor.com one last time, and *wham-o,* there it was: an attractive-looking two-story in our price range *and* in our neighborhood! Before my very eyes, there stood a homey-looking white house with green shutters and an upstairs balcony that ran the length of the place. It was faintly reminiscent of some of the quaint homes we had been used to seeing when we lived on the East Coast.

"Scott, come here!" I called out to my husband, who came running, wiping his hands on a dish towel. I tapped the photo on the computer screen excitedly while barking orders. "Grab your phone. Tell them we can be there in five minutes. I'll help the girls get dressed!"

On the way over, I began to worry that we might still need that cash-filled envelope after all. Or at least a pan of brownies. However, with no time to prepare a proper bribe, I instructed the girls as if I were a stage mother and we were headed to a group audition.

"Now listen to me," I coached. "When you meet the owner, smile, girls, smile! Don't say anything negative about *anything*. Do not mention that the dogs sometimes get indigestion. And don't ask if she requires a pet deposit for the hamster." In a low moment, I threatened to take the hamster for a one-way drive in the country. He was cute but not pet-deposit material.

I don't know if you've noticed this, but when it comes to photos of homes and real estate agents, there can be a shocking difference between what you see in the picture and what you see in person. I remember meeting one agent who looked more like her grandmother than the woman in her publicity photo. I think the photo was twenty years old, or altered, or she actually sent her grandmother to meet with us. Well, the same thing often applies to pictures of homes—all faded paint, cracks, and crabgrass appear to have been expertly airbrushed out—and the house only looks vaguely like the marketing photos.

The Perfect House?

As we pulled up to the house, it looked nice enough—but not nearly as eye-popping as the photo. The white paint and shutters needed a power wash, and dark and dirty screens on the large front windows were less than inviting. Grass, weeds, and potholes littered a lawn that badly needed mowing. That said, mature trees lined the street of well-maintained homes, and the location was great— in the same school zone as the kids' current school. *Thank You, Jesus!* I prayed silently. *One less major adjustment for the girls to handle along with starting a new school year.*

The house had been built in the 1980s, and it must have really loved that decade, because many parts were still living in the Reagan era. As we entered the front door, we were met by a musty odor and a beaming landlady about my age. "Come on in!" she greeted, wiping her brow and adjusting her tool belt. "I'm renovating the kitchen right now," she informed us, "but feel free to look around."

As it turned out, this landlady was a do-it-yourselfer extraordinaire and pointed out some impressive tile she had laid in the large great room. On the way to the kitchen, she pointed to the guest bathroom. "The cabinet's coming out, and I'm putting in a new sink and faucet." I silently thanked God for that bit of good news as well. The sink fixture appeared to be original to the house—brown wood with peeling bits of stain and chunky cut-glass knobs so large it would take the palms of a professional basketball player to operate them.

As we made our way to the kitchen, it began to sink in that this house was overdue for significant attention: The cabinets, countertops, sink fixtures, and stove needed to be replaced. Obviously, Our Lady of the Tool Belt had just begun, and we only had two weeks before we had to vacate our house. The more we toured, the more uneasy we became.

Upstairs, more musty odors greeted us and more NBA regulation-sized knobs. Around the edges of the bathroom floor, the linoleum was curling up from long-term duty. In the bedrooms, original cream-colored paint on the doors and baseboards showed signs of age, having turned a mustard-tinged shade of yellow. As for the good news, the carpet was in very good condition and the rooms were very large compared to newer homes. And when I glanced toward the ceiling-to-floor windows, I could see huge oak trees in the yard across the street.

Meanwhile, the girls had embarked on their own inspection.

"Hey guys, check this out!" Whitney yelled, but it took us a while to find her, hiding away in a niche under the stairs—it would make a great hideout for our youngest or a warm home for our kitty on winter nights.

From that moment on, she was sold. The rest of us were not so sure. Still, we were mindful of how hard it had been to find something we could afford in our town, so we indicated strong interest to the landlady. She graciously didn't press us for a deposit and even gave us her word that she would keep us first on her list. After so many weeks at the bottom of so many lists, this was a big plus. But we had to carefully consider the minuses to see if this equation was going to work out for us.

Over the weekend, we looked at a few homes in other areas. Days later, we came back to the one in our neighborhood to see how the updates were coming along. We were flat-footed with amazement. The kitchen had been transformed by new tile, granite countertops,

and cream-colored painted cabinets with new pulls. A
few key walls had also received a fresh coat of paint.
Most sinks sported new faucets and hardware suited
to average-sized hands. And the downstairs half bath
near the kitchen—the one with the dreadful old brown
cabinets—had been transformed into a charming space
reminiscent of a boutique hotel. I began to feel that this
house could be our new home. Our remarkable landlady
had proved to be a woman of her word, and then some.
So, with a feeling of great relief, we gathered around a
countertop and signed a lease.

Later that night, I sat up in bed, wide awake. I
wondered, *After all our prayer and searching—have we made
the right choice?* The more I lay there second-guessing, the
more I knew I wasn't going back to sleep for a while.
My husband had fallen asleep watching TV in the next
room, so I decided to look over the school directory
to see which classmates might be our new neighbors.
Skimming the list of names from *A* to *E* without seeing
a familiar one, I became a little concerned.

"Hmmm," I said. "No one near us yet. I guess most
of them live in the new development across from our
school." But when I had reached the *K*s, concern gave
way to nervousness. "Wow," I muttered as the darkness
outside gave way to dawn, "that's odd—not one family

lives near the house we just rented." When I reached the *W*s, my heart sank. I spoke out loud, forgetting about sleepers near and far: "Oh my goodness. Did the zone lines change? Surely not!"

I threw off the covers and raced to the computer in the office, pulling up the boundary map, squinting hard to see the tiny street names. Guess what? The boundaries *had* changed. We were one street off from the girls' current school. "One street off!" I uttered in disbelief.

I didn't know whether to laugh or cry. I was worried how Tori and Whitney would handle the news. And to all you rule benders out there—no, there was no wiggle room allowed at the old school, no benevolent administrator cooing, "Oh, we mustn't lose your wonderful girls. Of *course* they can stay. The place just wouldn't be the same without them." No, I was a fly-by-the-seat-of-my-pants mother faced with a by-the-book school district.

Given the arduous journey to finding a nice home in our price range, I accepted this news as the will of God—and prayed the girls would do the same. Tori, our oldest, took the word like a champ. At first, she seemed slightly worried about the unknown, yet she was reassured that we'd be in the same neighborhood near familiar friends. Whitney, upbeat by nature, surprised me by bursting into tears. After a long hug and a relatively short but uncomfortably intense cry, she seemed game to give it a go.

Which brings me back to those two little words that pack a punch: We moved.

· · · · · · · · If There's One Thing You · · · · · · · · · Can Count On—It's Change

We lived with floor-to-ceiling boxes—painstakingly unpacking and decluttering ten years of Polly Pocket accessories (earrings the size of sugar ants, purses the size of Chicklet gum) and enough Build-A-Bear stuffed animals with designer clothing to cover a month's rent even if sold at garage sale prices. We also dealt with the sheer exhaustion of tackling myriad tasks while at the same time retraining our brains to the quirks of our new surroundings. For example, we couldn't get the fridge through the front door, so we accessed it from the garage for two weeks. On occasion I still find myself standing beside the car with an empty glass, looking for the milk carton.

For the first time in my life, I had some idea of how a raw chicken feels when dropped into a bag of Shake 'N Bake. Only instead of seasonings flying at me willy-nilly, it was all the *stuff* I'd accumulated. The parade of belongings felt endless. In that first month, I looked like the same person on the outside, but on the inside. . .whew. I think "mental vertigo" is the term I'm looking for here.

The girls indeed had to change schools, which may not be the worst thing in the world—but it's never comfortable to be the new kid. It's tough working the hallways and lunch table without your familiar peeps, not being known as the stellar human being you were in your old haunt. But still, God has used it—a little humility never hurt anyone. Often it helps develop character in the long run.

So Tori and Whitney are learning new lessons of empathy for new kids—or for any kid who is not like all the rest, since the school also serves mentally and physically challenged kids, some of whom have captured my girls' hearts. The student body is a bit more racially diverse, which has expanded the girls' outlook on life beyond their own little world, as well.

These are new experiences that no doubt help the girls choose gratitude when they're tempted to feel sorry for themselves. They're blessed with enthusiastic and savvy teachers and are slowly making new friends. A few months into things, my shy Tori came out of her shell and gave a standout speech for which her classmates selected her to be their student council representative— she's finding that she enjoys swimming in a smaller, different pond for a while. My girls are also learning— at the ripe old ages of nine and eleven—that God is still good, and that He is "for" them in uncomfortable and challenging situations.

It's been a month now since the move, and things are feeling close to normal again. The only weird thing is that, all of a sudden, I've turned into my neat-freak husband. With my brain on overload, I knew that in order to think straight, I *had* to have a plan for dealing with our daily stuff. And I realized that since my kids were no longer little, we might actually have a shot at keeping the house neatish. So I'm marching around, like Oscar-Madison-turned-Felix-Unger, barking: "A place for everything and everything in its place!" After picking up a dozen pairs of socks and unmentionables off the girls' bedroom floors, my motto became, "A place for everything or look for your clothes on the front lawn!"

Another weird phenomenon: Our furniture, purchased new twenty years ago from Ethan Allen, had become symbolic of the changes in my body and life over the same period of time. The once pristine cherry case goods and wingback chairs upholstered in designer fabrics were now dotted with stains, scratches, rips, and scars. Children, dogs, and three moves had taken their toll.

Running my hand along a particularly deep scratch in our dining room chair, my thoughts turned back to a time when the chair and I were in our prime. I was thirty and had a mentor in her fifties, a woman who encouraged me to nurture my relationship with Jesus and face life's hard questions head-on with Him.

I remember having coffee at a local bakery and studying Prior's face, thinking, *Wow, that's interesting—she has some wrinkles, some gray hair, some age spots, but fiftysomething looks good on her*. I loved visiting Prior's cottage-style home in Norfolk, Virginia. It was white, weathered, and not well air-conditioned in summer—as was common in that part of the country. I think the scarcity of artificial air had something to do with the natural look that I admired about Prior—no plentiful A/C to keep one's hair and makeup pristine all day. Her furniture was well worn and comfortable, dressed in intriguing shades of faded coral, slate blue, and grey toile fabrics. The living room lovingly hosted pictures of her sons as white-blond toddlers, later turned strapping young teens, and finally college graduates. Prior's life had seemed so different to me then—so mature—so very far off from the one I was living at the time.

But today, after taking a good look at my own furniture and body, I realized that *I've* turned into that mature, natural woman. In some ways, it feels like a rite of passage. In others, like a kick in the teeth. I'm no longer the one with the brand-new house, brand-new furniture, and brand-new kids. I'm the slightly bohemian older woman living on a tight budget in a quirky rental house with faded and scratched furniture, inhabiting a body showing undeniable signs of wear and tear.

For the most part, I'm at peace with this life transition, coming on the heels of having lived ten years in Texas. I like that I can look back to see how God has mellowed me in ways—how He redeemed some of my immature behaviors and naive decisions. I've not "arrived," whatever that means. (I hope it doesn't mean "arrived on the platform waiting for the Glory Train.") But it's nice to be at a place where I can look back and see some internal maturity that came with the external scratches and dents. Perhaps that's not a bad price to pay for youth lost.

Still, on occasion, I feel a twinge of longing for "what was." I miss the fresh look my body and furnishings once had. But God even encourages me there. At open house at the girls' new school, for instance, I realized to my delight that I'd been roaming the halls for a good fifteen minutes before I felt that old pang of inferiority when eyeballing the younger, hipper moms. It seemed there were a good number of older moms at this school, more than at the previous one, and I felt a little more at home.

And so, God—true to form—continues to move in mysterious ways. And our family is moving on with Him. We've learned so much about each other, the nature of transitions, and God's faithfulness with us, every shaky step of the way. It's a good feeling now to be thankful for where we are and looking forward to the future.

If you're facing unsettling changes, this is a great time to hone a life-affirming outlook. Contrary to what you might expect, that does not come naturally to me. But I've been learning that my *thoughts* greatly impact my *feelings*, so that's always a good place to start— working on a positive take on things in my head.

May you, too, hold tight to faith more often than you give in to fear. May you turn to laughter more often than to tears. And, most of all, may you find that God is for you, even when life as you've known it is. . . moving on.

By nature we like the familiar
and dislike the strange.[1]

MAIMONIDES

· ·

The future ain't what it used to be.[2]
ATTRIBUTED TO YOGI BERRA, PAUL VALERY,
AND CASEY STENGEL

Reflections on Your Well-Lived Laugh—
Designing a Life That Keeps You Smiling

1) On a scale of 1 (being lowest) to 10 (the highest), how much does the pressure of change bother you?

2) What are two or three words that describe how you feel about this pressure now?

3) What are two or three words that describe how you would feel if this pressure were lessened or removed?

4) Looking at your answers 1–3, on a scale of 1 to 10, how motivated are you to reduce this pressure?

5) Who is someone with whom you feel emotionally safe—who will encourage you while you decide how best to reduce this pressure?

6) Use this space to write some thoughts or feelings that this pressure has brought to your mind.

7) If this pressure negatively impacts your life in a significant way, try finishing this sentence:
I want to live well, laugh often, and smile more! I can begin by choosing to take this one step. . .

8
The Emotional Lives of Women

❧

The Pressure of Emotions

I've often felt that referring to a baby boy as a "bundle of joy" was an apt analogy. But baby girls? I think the phrase "bundle of emotions" is often more accurate. If you're of the female species, maybe you can relate. Emotions, it seems, come inseparably packaged with hormones and the nurturing nature—and they can be a long-term challenge for many of us.

Not long ago, I was reminded how starkly different women can be regarding how and where they express their feelings. I, being a more creative type and a Texan from a long line of back-slapping, welcoming kin, tend to be on the boisterous and open side of the communication spectrum. My experience living in Virginia, however, taught me—often the hard way—that there are plenty of women who are more conversationally careful and emotionally reserved.

Somehow this helpful realization slipped my mind as I took it upon myself to offer a hearty Texas welcome to an East Coast woman in her fifties. She was new to a book club I'd been attending (in which I knew only one other woman, and not well), so I offered to sit next to her at the first meeting. On subsequent meetings, we often sat near each other and exchanged small talk.

Over the course of several meetings, I joined in the discussion by sharing some observations of the chapters we were reviewing. At times my insights were heartfelt, even vulnerable. It had seemed to me that my observations were well received—there were nodding heads, chuckles, even a few women dabbing at their teary eyes with a tissue. After all, we were *women* discussing a novel about love and loss.

After the third meeting, the newcomer leaned over and whispered, "May I speak privately with you for a moment?"

"Sure," I answered, thinking, *Boy, the discussion must have hit a nerve with her tonight; and here she is all alone with no one to talk to, being the new kid on the block.* Having been in that position in the past, my heart went out to her— and I was ready to lend an empathetic ear and a pre-moistened lotion tissue, if necessary.

As we found our way to an anteroom and settled into wingback chairs, I tried to ease the tension I felt *she* felt, by asking, "Is something wrong?" The woman sat straight up as if at attention, looked me squarely in the eye, and said matter-of-factly, "I offer this in kindness. But I think you should know that people don't really care to know how you *feel* about everything—it's far too much information to process. I've learned it's best to keep emotions close to the vest and would ask you to consider doing the same." All of the sudden the tables were turned: *I* felt like the outsider in need of an empathetic ear and a high-tech tissue.

I know I'm sounding like a hypersensitive creative type, but I hope you'll indulge me as I describe how this woman's advice made me *feel*. Her words stung my heart like a deranged hornet then stuck to it like hot globs of tar from freshly laid blacktop. My mind kept replaying her cutting admonishment: *I've learned it's best to keep emotions close to the vest and would ask you to consider doing the same.* I tried to brush off her words, like irritating dandruff on a black trench coat—but I could feel them weaving havoc into the fabric of my soul.

The whole unpleasant affair had me questioning how I relate to others.

Who Am I?

Not long after this disorienting interchange, our family traveled from Texas to the University of Michigan in Ann Arbor to see our son portray the lovable old schoolmaster Mr. Lundie in the musical *Brigadoon*. I hardly recognized Trevor as he walked on stage with the aid of a cane, wearing a strikingly realistic white wig and moustache that had been hand-woven by a professional wig maker from New York. Mr. Lundie began softly speaking in a Scottish dialect, "Aye, lads and lassies, it's time for a weddin'." And then, with a twinkly wink of his eye, the audience was spirited away to "Bree-ga-dewn"—a mystical town teeming with kilted clansmen, bagpipers, and maidens gathering the heather that grows wild on the hillside.

That weekend, I set up an appointment on campus to order photographs from the production. As I stepped into the small music theater office, a woman behind a desk popped up eagerly to greet me, "Welcome!" she said as she extended her hand. "You must be Trevor's mom. We just love Trevor! Follow me—you can view photos over here."

I took a seat near a man who appeared to be the father of another music theater student. He was fixated on a computer screen showing about a hundred dreamy images of *Brigadoon* in brilliant colors.

This could take a while, I thought. *He seems pretty engrossed in those photos.*

With time to kill, my mind drifted off to a place that is often not pleasant: Introspection Isle. Even on this glorious getaway, my heart still radiated with residual pain whenever my mind wandered back to that close-to-the-vest book club woman who insinuated that I was wrong to freely express my feelings. *She has a point,* I mentally scolded myself. *Not everyone cares to know how I feel. . . . I should be more sensitive. How could I be so immature?*

I had just about convinced myself to grow up when the father who had been reviewing photos pushed his chair back from the screen, turned to me, and smiled, his eyes brimming with tears. "I'm a mess," he said, shaking his head while throwing up his hands toward heaven. "I want to buy them *all*—this is my daughter's last performance before moving to New York." Then, shaking his head in quiet disbelief, he added, "Let me tell you, it goes so fast. *So* fast."

My own eyes moistened—not only with empathy for how he was feeling, but also for how, in the blink of an eye shedding a spontaneous tear, I felt the healing power of connection and validation that comes when one human being openly shares feelings with a stranger. I flew back to Introspective Isle, but this time it was a good head trip. *I'm a writer,* I thought. *I'm an artist by heart, and I feel most at home with people like this father.*

• • • • • • • • • • It's Okay to be *You* • • • • • • • • • • •

Over the years, people have used a smattering of intriguing words to describe me. Some words I like.

Others, not so much. Adjectives like *hilarious* and *endearing* melt in my soul like cotton candy on my tongue—so sweet, so satisfying. But words like *intense* and *loud* stick in my brain like red candy apple on my dental work.

Maybe you know how I feel. *Every* personality has its upsides and downsides. I'm not suggesting we should all communicate in the same way, just that whether you're a close-to-the-vester or an open-booker, most women possess an emotional river deep within. Knowing how best to navigate the troubled waters of that reservoir can be tricky—like nailing Jell-O to the proverbial wall.

Looking back on my life, I often think how liberating it would have been to be emotionally mature at the ripe old age of, say, twenty. How amazing it would have been to have my emotional house in order before I went to college, got married, and had my first child. Just think of the heartache I could have avoided. Mark Twain put it this way: "Life would be infinitely happier if we could only be born at the age of eighty and gradually approach eighteen."

Whoever said "youth is wasted on the young" must have shared the fantasy of possessing the wisdom of the ages while still looking underage. Imagine having the wisdom of someone in her fifties, like Billy Graham's daughter, Anne Graham Lotz, while looking like personal trainer Jillian Michaels. Nobody gets that luxury, except maybe Beth Moore. And she's been kind enough to help hoist us out of our pits and wave so long to our insecurities, so it's hard to be jealous of her. What would being jealous get us anyway, except maybe a run-in with a lightning bolt on a dark, rainy night in the parking lot of a Women of Faith Conference.

While there *are* plenty of "mature" women who are attractive and wise, very few get to be young and profoundly wise. The exceptions may be those young women who have suffered life-altering tragedies that have a way of forging "wisdom beyond one's years."

But most of us must cut our wisdom teeth, so to speak, over time and many experiences. The good news? The more disastrous our choices, the more wisdom we stand to gain if we'll learn from the heartache that ensues. This had my brain wondering, *With good news like this, who needs bad news?*

During my early thirties, I realized the consequences of how I handled my emotions had ratcheted up a couple of notches—my reactions no longer just affected only me. I had passed through the carefree era of singleness into the semicarefree era of DINK (double income, no kids), then set sail for the mother land:

suburban housewife with kid. I may have been emoting for one, but all three of us would feel the aftershocks if I overreacted to certain stressors.

As the two men in my life (one big, one little) pushed buttons that turned me from Andy Griffith's Aunt Bea to the Wicked Witch of the East in the wink of a flying monkey's eyelash, I suddenly needed to know if Emmanuel—"God with Us"—had to deal with people and circumstances that drove Him nuts, too. More to the point, I wondered if I was a complete disappointment to God-with-Me when I lost my temper or made mountains out of ant piles.

I remember the winter night I set out to make my first chili dinner. Grocery list in hand, I painstakingly selected each ingredient: ground round, spices, vine-ripened tomatoes, celery, and onions. Cooking is not my thing, but I was a young wife and mother determined to give it my best shot. *Who knows?* I thought. *Maybe I'll awaken a chef within if I just assemble the perfect ingredients and get them percolating.* (In case you're wondering about the use of that verb, I *did* know enough not to cook chili in the coffeepot.)

As the pot bubbled on my stove top, three-year-old Trevor sat by the sink fiddling with a lime-green sponge, contentedly observing my culinary endeavor with the detached disinterest one would expect from a boy his age. As the aroma of chili powder and stewed tomatoes began wafting through the air, I realized I needed to set the table before my husband arrived.

"Mommy will be back in a sec," I called to Trevor as I stepped into the dining room to put out the silverware. When I returned, Trevor was no longer sitting happily by the sink fingering a sponge; instead, he was standing on the counter, clutching a bottle of Ajax cleaner, and spritzing my cabinets. Liquid cleaner ran down the white doors, dripping like sudsy raindrops into the chili pot.

I wish I could say at that moment that I was still able to see the humor and laugh it off. I *wish* I could say that. Instead, I grabbed Trevor around the waist with what must have felt to him like superhuman strength, and let loose a few, shall we say, *poorly chosen* angry words. Then I marched him down the hall and unceremoniously deposited my perplexed son on his bed, slamming the door behind me—the exclamation point to my outburst.

Heart racing, its beating pounding audibly in my ears, I returned to the scene of the crime and dumped the ruined chili down the disposal as tears spilled down my cheeks. It was one of those times when a mother knows she's raced past the yellow line of wish-I-hadn't-done-that and skidded into the red zone of regret—and it's too late to shift into reverse. I stood at the sink, awash in self-loathing.

I don't want to be like this! I thought. *For Trevor's sake, for Scott's sake. . .for* my *sake. I can't react like this—even to something this upsetting. I've got to get a grip on my emotions.*

Mercifully, a few minutes later, Trevor forgave me for my inappropriate anger, and I forgave him for behaving like a three-year-old left alone with a spray bottle. And we made corn dogs for dinner together.

That was the end of my chili-making career, and Trevor developed a phobia of spray bottles that has kept our relationship running like a well-oiled machine ever since.

That fateful evening was a gift—an epiphany. And isn't that the best outcome of our worst moments? Healing epiphanies are God's redemptive power to overcome. Shortly after that experience, I began a journey of self-discovery and the healing of those "child-within" wounds we all seem to carry into adulthood—the ones that so often surface when we have children of our own. As singer Alanis Morrisette puts it, "We carry on our back the burden time always reveals."

My father helped me understand that the best use

of regret is to convert it into motivation to change. "Once you make the decision 'Never again,'" he kindly said, "make a plan, set a course, and don't look back." In terms of moving toward *positive action* versus *negative reaction*, I began to work a plan that involved reminding myself that some reactions were just "too costly"—and I should avoid them at all costs. Even now, I still actively work at managing my feelings and reactions to stress-arousing circumstances. It's not been easy, but over time I've seen much progress. . .as have those who know me well.

· · · · · · · · · Jesus Was Emotional, Too · · · · · · · · ·

Yes, handling emotions well is an ongoing process for many women. To be sure, there are those who are more even tempered by nature (though they have other battles—I've learned no one gets off the hook completely). I've admired these more naturally easygoing women and have determined to learn from them.

One time, watching a mellower friend unloading her dishwasher while calmly and delicately removing the serrated blade of a steak knife from her toddler's clenched fist, I was dumbfounded that she never skipped a beat in our conversation or changed her tone of voice with the child. Mission accomplished, with no drama or injury. It was one of those moments that made an impression on me, and I still take mental notes when I see women handle difficult situations with emotional poise. (Note: I wanted to use the word *sangfroid* instead of *poise*, but my editor said it sounded pretentious. Then I said, "True. But it's more fun to say.")

Of course, we tend to think Jesus was perfectly sangfroid, right? Up until my early and exhausting child-rearing days, it was easy for me to think of Jesus as being *half* human, not *really* human—kind of like the bubble boy who lives in a sterile environment because if he engaged with anyone outside his plasticized room, the germs would kill him instantly. Jesus' humanity hadn't really been a big deal to me. But somehow having a little person relying on me to help him with everything from wiping his bum to holding his chewed gum, I started to wonder how Jesus, being perfect, could interact with me, sooo imperfect, without disintegrating on the spot.

As I read Philip Yancy's book *The Jesus I Never Knew*, I came to realize that Jesus was a real person who experienced the full range of human emotions. He was completely without sin and with the purest of motivations—but I don't believe that necessarily lessened the intensity of His feelings.

As a hormonal, emotional being, I feel it is important to contemplate the idea that Jesus felt emotions like euphoria and despair—and felt them at full impact, just as *I* might. This realization was hugely comforting. It served as a pivotal point of connection with Christ as the Great Friend (as the timeless devotional *God Calling* refers to Him) at a time when I really needed a great friend.

I finally felt I had a comrade who understood the emotional minefield I was walking as a too-often-overwhelmed young mother and wife.

Englishman John Stott, an Anglican rector and scholar, had a similar revelation:

> *I discovered. . .that Jesus of Nazareth, the perfect human being, was no tight-lipped, unemotional ascetic. On the contrary, I read that he turned on hypocrites with anger, looked on a rich young ruler and loved him, could both rejoice in spirit and sweat drops of blood in spiritual agony, was constantly moved with compassion, and even burst into tears twice in public. From all this evidence it is plain that our emotions are not to be suppressed, since they have an essential place in our humanness and therefore in our Christian discipleship.*[1]

Think of it: Scripture indicates that while Jesus was fully God, He was at the same time *fully human.* Think of the most alive, fully human person you know—and, well, Jesus was probably something like that person. The most fully human people I know are the most endearing people I know. They've been chewed up and spit out by life pain. They have nothing to prove, except perhaps that their lives have become much more about what God wants and much less about their own demands and plans. They aren't afraid to express their human emotions—laughter, tears, tenderness, fear, anger, you name it. They've also learned the hard lessons of reactionary behavior and vigilantly avoid spewing harsh words and out-of-control emotions on others.

It's not that these fully-human folks are nearly perfect. Not at all. It's more that they empathize with the pain of others—having been through it themselves—and they've made loving relationships an at-all-costs priority.

Jesus is a lot like that. How could He not be? It cost Him everything to relate to us and then to save us from the penalty of death. When I think about Jesus' Jewishness, I'm reminded of the Jewish folks I have met who are animated communicators with big hearts. They were perceptive, fun loving, and loyal. There are of course exceptions to any generality, but this has been my observation and experience. I like to think of Jesus that way—an engaging, fun, deeply thoughtful Jewish man, or God-man, in this case.

Think of the gospel account of the woman who—in an emotional extravaganza—wept and poured out an entire vial of costly perfume on Jesus' feet. The disciples subtly belittled her by suggesting the money for that perfume could have been put to more logical use—even more *spiritual* use (feeding the poor). But Jesus stood up for the woman, saying, "It is a beautiful thing she has done!" He elevated her gift from the heart, complimenting her further by comparing *her* tender ministry to His needs with what the *disciples* had done to welcome Him, which was. . .oh yeah. . .nothing. Then he told them, "This woman will be remembered for this." And she was, because here I am writing about it two thousand years later.

If you, too, are an emotive woman—if you've ever doubted that Jesus understands and values your heart-on-sleeve outpouring—this story should soothe you. He values your heart gifts—your tears, your joy, your impassioned words of love and admiration—even if it seems illogical to others who aren't wired for passionate public expression.

If you're a close-to-the-vest woman by nature, this

discussion may hold little interest. You may be perfectly content for your emotions to show only in the private company of one (or a tight circle of a few). Many great women prefer this—including some who have been dynamic leaders in world history—so you are in good company. But if you find yourself desiring more emotional depth in your relationships with others or Christ, perhaps this chapter will be fodder for thought. In keeping with the goal of this book, to each her own.

Now, if you'll excuse me, this emotional girl has a sunset to savor, a kid to laugh with, and a Hallmark commercial to cry over.

There are only two ways to live your life. One is as though nothing is a miracle. The other is as though everything is a miracle.[2]

ALBERT EINSTEIN

. . . .

But are not this struggle and even the mistakes one may make better, and do they not develop us more, than if we kept systematically away from emotions?[3]

VINCENT VAN GOGH

Reflections on Your Well-Lived Laugh—
Designing a Life That Keeps You Smiling

1) On a scale of 1 (being lowest) to 10 (the highest), how much does the pressure of emotions bother you?

2) What are two or three words that describe how you feel about this pressure now?

3) What are two or three words that describe how you would feel if this pressure were lessened or removed?

4) Looking at your answers 1–3, on a scale of 1 to 10, how motivated are you to reduce this pressure?

5) Who is someone with whom you feel emotionally safe—who will encourage you while you decide how best to reduce this pressure?

6) Use this space to write some thoughts or feelings that this pressure has brought to your mind.

7) If this pressure negatively impacts your life in a significant way, try finishing this sentence:
I want to live well, laugh often, and smile more! I can begin by choosing to take this one step. . .

9
Friending (and Unfriending)

❧

The Pressure of "BFF"

If you're a Facebook fan, you've likely experienced the high of having about a hundred people flood your inbox with friend requests. Ah. . .the euphoria of feeling like the captain of the cheerleading team. It seems just about everyone wants to be your BFF.

But if you've been a Facebook junkie for long, you've probably had the unpleasant experience of logging onto your account and realizing you've suddenly gone AWOL on a friend's account. That can take you from a prom queen high to an odd-one-out low in no time.

For most women, this is the nature of friendship: we are friended and unfriended several times over our lifetime. Most friends come into our lives for a season, and though friendships may last for years—sometimes a great number of years—few last a lifetime. That's because friendships, like the people who make them, are influenced by a lot of factors, some of which can solidify a connection or become its undoing.

· · · · · · · · · Friends for All Seasons · · · · · · · · · ·

Looking back, most of my friendships were seasonal— formed during a particular time in my life: high school, college, MWOK (married without kids), and MWK (married with kids). That trend continues—I tend to make friendships based on where I spend most of my time.

Some of the funniest, easy-to-be-with women I've had the pleasure of befriending came from the time I worked at a graduate university in Virginia. I was in my twenties; at first single then married. I shared cozy seafood dinners on the Chesapeake Bay with some, played riotous rounds of the game Outburst with others, attended equestrian matches with others, and discussed the trials of young love over lunch with still others.

The drawback was this: Since this was a *graduate* school, many of my kismet friends left in a matter of two short years. Saying "so long" left a little hole in my heart each time.

One particularly rough May, an unusual number of friends graduated and immediately left the area: a business school major moved to England, a biblical studies buddy became a missionary to China, a public policy friend moved to Washington, D.C., and several headed to various other U.S. destinations. I remember thinking, *I don't know how many more good-byes I have in me.*

Thankfully, not long after that bumper crop of movers and shakers flew the coop, I was ruling the roost at home with a new baby. In my life as a stay-at-home mom, I found—to my great relief and joy—new, fantastically fun and loving friends who were raising little chicks of their own. I learned that as one season of life gave way to the next, some friendships faded and new ones began.

Fillers and Drainers

Like everything else in life, our friendships are seen through the lens of our unique perspective—our personality, preferences, and past experiences. One friend wrote that she finds some friends fill our emotional tank; others drain it. She was insightful enough to realize that when she feels her energy being drained, it says as much about *her* as it does the other person. She knows what she can handle well and what she can't at that time in her life:

> *We inevitably find that there are people who fill our tanks and drain our tanks. Bella is a filler for me. No matter what is going on in her life, she always asks how I am doing and seems to hang on every word as I answer. She's an optimistic, easy laugher—things that really fill my tank.*

Denise is a young mom of two preschool girls who is in that navel-gazing stage of introspection many of us go through at her age. I love her dearly, but it's become impossible to talk at the depth she desires because of the kids' constant interruptions.

Eventually I encouraged her to see a life coach, and now she's getting the focused attention and direction she craves—and we're free to hang out with no agenda but to relax and have fun.

Another friend wrote me this fabulous piece of advice, especially helpful for those who struggle with overextending themselves for the drainers in their lives:

I'm learning that we are responsible to *people, not responsible* for *people. We can acknowledge pain, respond in a timely manner to a text, e-mail, or phone call, but we are not responsible to fix people or their problems.*

• • • • • • Go Where You Are Celebrated, • • • • • • Not Where You Are Tolerated

As I mentioned in another chapter, when choosing relationships, it's a good idea to go where we are celebrated, not tolerated. If you've ever invested significant time struggling to fit in with a particular circle of women, only to find out later you were a perfect, easy match with a different group, you know what I mean. Ironically, the very characteristics that drain our tank may be the same characteristics that fill someone else's.

Take a look at these opposing perspectives, for example:

- One woman's needy is another's vulnerable.
- One woman's chatty is another's conversationalist.
- One woman's indecisive is another's serendipitous.
- One woman's stoic is another's tough cookie.
- One woman's scatterbrained is another's free spirit.
- One woman's rude is another's direct.
- One woman's odd is another's unconventional.
- One woman's overthinker is another's insightful.
- One woman's inflexible is another's consistent.
- One woman's inappropriate humor is another's edgy humor.

And the list goes on and on and on.

Perhaps when we're tempted to define someone in a negative light, we should remind ourselves that *our* defining characteristics can be viewed as positive or negative depending on *who* is doing the evaluating. My grandmother used to say, "There ain't no accountin' for taste." When it comes to friendship, grandma makes an astute observation.

• • • • • • You Say Tomato, I Say Tomahto; • • • • • • Let's Make Tomato-Tomahto Soup

As I reflect on my own current circles of friendship, I realize that my innermost group is comprised of a few women I've know from eight to twenty-eight years. These folks are my go-to peeps—the ones with whom I most want to share my joys and sorrows, and on whom I can rely to pray for me. I also consider my mother, father, and sister among my closest friends and confidants.

Interestingly, my sister Becky enjoys a close friendship with her adult daughter, Rachel Praise, so maybe friending progeny runs in our family. There are no doubt countless crazy episodes like the one that follows that have helped solidify Becky's friendship with her grown-up daughter. This comforts me, because as much as my young daughters feign protest about my goofiness and ineptitude, they are quick to remind me that the laughter we share on a daily basis is a highlight in their lives.

The following is an excerpt from Becky's book, a peek into the life of extreme personality differences. Becky is go-with-the-flow, RP is all-about-the-plan—yet it ends up somehow. . .working.

After a most pleasant trip to Nashville with Rachel Praise when she was a teen, a most unpleasant thing happened at the airport on our way back to Dallas: my suitcase exploded. I had stuffed it with loot from an outlet mall, and it finally succumbed to the pressure of one too many clearance priced lace bras. As I wrapped my burgeoning bag with yards of duct tape, I caught a glimpse of Rachel in the distance, nodding and smiling in my direction as if to say to passersby, "I wonder who that poor imbecile is?"

We made the trip back to Dallas without a hitch, and my daughter agreed to walk by my side once again. However, as we entered the parking garage, I could not for the life of me remember where I had parked my car.

We spent the next two hours searching rows of

parked cars, pushing and pulling three large rolling
suitcases (one almost completely covered in duct tape—
hey I couldn't risk losing those cheap lace bras—so I
figured if a little tape is good, more is better.)

Finally, I devised a strategy in which I would leave
Rachel by our pile of suitcases while I ran back and forth
looking for our car. Then we'd haul the baggage down
a few more yards, and she'd luggage-sit while I sprinted
and searched again.

Upon returning from one of my search and run
missions, I found my tired daughter sitting atop the taped
luggage looking like the orphan on the Les Miserables
poster, soberly munching on what appeared to be a cookie.

"Honey," I asked, "where'd you get that?"

"A lady just walked by and said I looked like I could
use a cookie." Rachel breathed a sigh of exasperation as
she put her head in her hands. "Mom, she thought I was
homeless."

When they got to the car, the battery was dead because
Becky had left the lights on. At this point, Rachel's
ability to find humor in their situation was at an all-time
low. But Becky, trying to renew her daughter's resolve
to buck up, said, "Don't worry. We'll figure this out.
We're a team. Like Helen Keller and Annie Sullivan or
Thelma and Louise!"

To which Rachel deadpanned, "Or Dumb and Dumber."

So I've learned from example that bonds can be formed from very different personalities—as long as there's lots of acceptance, compromise, and the ability to *not* take yourself (or your friend) too seriously.

· · · · · A Lifelong Look at Friendships · · · · · ·

My own mom, whom I've admired for her ability to make relationships and enjoy them thoroughly, has experienced the ups and downs of friendship for over seventy years now. I once wrote to her about the roles friends play in our lives, asking whether it had been worth it to keep making new friends, knowing they might be a part of her life for only a brief time— knowing that in parting, friends sometimes break your heart.

She wrote back:

Well. . .you ask a good question—because most friendships are often seasonal, does that make them any less important in one's life?

I've lived a long time now, in a number of situations

involving social clubs, women's ministry, church, and neighborhoods. After moving to Texas in my forties, I thought I'd die of loneliness there! Neighbors were situated close enough to spit a watermelon seed on and, sadly, turned out not to be worth the spit and the seed even if I tried—we had the equivalent of the Hatfields and McCoys on either side of us during that crazy time.

I've learned over these seventy-plus years that we humans truly are fearfully and wonderfully made, yet at the same time, we all *have our weaknesses that make us, well, a little nutso at times. I've learned not to expect someone to be even* close *to perfect.*

Interestingly, the one friend I had during that time was a doll, and we hit it off. But she was popular and sought-after and already committed to women with whom she'd been through lots of life dramas together. So when I moved ten years later, the friendship faded, and I think that was okay with both of us.

As to lifelong friends, they are few for me but cherished. Your uncle James had the good sense to marry my best friend from grade school—your aunt Martha. She's the one whom, in our teens, I wrestled with over a chicken leg during a late night snack in the kitchen. It ended with us laughing to tears and sitting on the floor exchanging bites. We still laugh 'til we cry sometimes, but we've had to put the wrestling matches on hold.

Then there was the friend I had for many, many years while raising you kiddos, and I thought I'd never lose her. But I did, despite several efforts to restore the relationship. I had great affection for her and found her interesting and entertaining. Our struggles were so different (we had money, they were always strapped; I was happily married, and she, much less so; my kids were well-adjusted, and hers struggled). So whether it was envy or feeling that I couldn't relate to her deepest needs—I'll never know. She fell ill about the time your dad and I retired and moved, so sheer logistics would have made it hard to see each other.

So, yes, there have been times when I felt like just forgetting making new friends. But I know I can't go it alone. I have come to view most friendships as sort of serial relationships, given by our Father for certain seasons or needs in life.

Friendships don't have to be forever if they fulfill the need of the time. This way we have the joy of getting to know lots more of God's kids than we might have otherwise. When we accept that most friendships will be transitory, it can make the partings less painful.

I agree with my mom—friendships *are* worth it. Though most of them will be seasonal, in those seasons they are vital emotional life ropes. A good friend for now, in *this* season, is an amazing gift to be cherished.

Each friend represents a world in us,
a world possibly not born until they
arrive, and it is only by this meeting
that a new world is born.[1]

ANAIS NIN

. . . .

Friendship is something that
raises us almost above humanity.
It is the sort of love one can
imagine between angels.[2]

C. S. LEWIS

Reflections on Your Well-Lived Laugh—
Designing a Life That Keeps You Smiling

1) On a scale of 1 (being lowest) to 10 (the highest), how much does the pressure of "BFF" bother you?

2) What are two or three words that describe how you feel about this pressure now?

3) What are two or three words that describe how you would feel if this pressure were lessened or removed?

4) Looking at your answers 1–3, on a scale of 1 to 10, how motivated are you to reduce this pressure?

5) Who is someone with whom you feel emotionally safe—who will encourage you while you decide how best to reduce this pressure?

6) Use this space to write some thoughts or feelings that this pressure has brought to your mind.

7) If this pressure negatively impacts your life in a significant way, try finishing this sentence:
I want to live well, laugh often, and smile more! I can begin by choosing to take this one step. . .

10

Party Poopers

The Pressure to Fix "It"

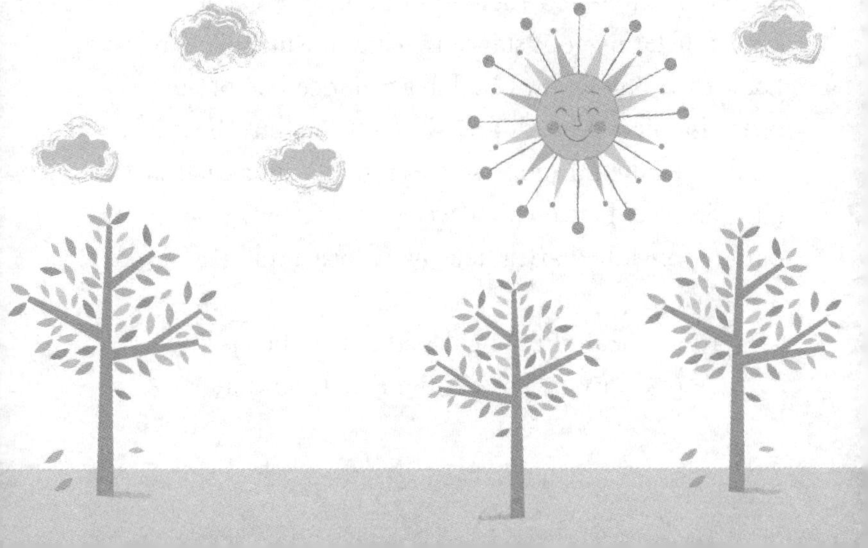

On a sunny day in late May, I stopped for breakfast at the Dream Café in a happening area of downtown Dallas. I'm a patsy for carbohydrates at daybreak, especially those that have been embellished—with roasted almonds, caramelized sugar, cream cheese—that sort of thing. And on this day, I'd fallen for granola-encrusted French toast that was a specialty of the house.

After savoring my fix, replete with real butter and Vermont syrup, I took a leisurely walk back to the car. I strolled past alfresco diners with their faces shaded by the *Dallas Morning News* and their feet nestled comfortably in canvas boat shoes.

I wandered past large clay pots filled with purple petunias, their heads looking like miniature Victrolas, and happened upon Sotheby's Realty. The sun bounced off the building's corrugated tin roof, showcasing a lineup of fat pigeons standing wing to wing, like River Dancers at the ready. I had never noticed before how beautiful pigeon heads are when the sun hits them just right. Metallic turquoise segues into dazzling fuchsia, glittering like handmade jewelry crafted by a gray-haired ponytailed artist, face like a peach pit, leathered by the sun.

"You're beautiful!" I chirped to the chorus line on the hot tin roof. "How come I've never noticed you before?" The birds, ruffled by the sound of my voice, began wobbling side to side like chubby Charlie Chaplins, talons clicking on their makeshift dance floor. Not wanting to disturb them further, I quietly continued walking.

A few steps farther along, I spied the calling cards of the dancing birds covering the sidewalk like white polka dots. And one was positioned squarely beneath my sandal, perilously close to my bare foot.

"*Yuuuck!* That is so disgusting!" I ranted, lifting my head toward the roof while wiping my sandal on some grass. The pigeons flew off, offering no apology—and I joined the throngs of people who find pigeons to be essentially icky.

Beautiful yet yucky. Amazing yet disgusting. Pigeons remind me that, in spite of the many things in our lives that are both beautiful and amazing—there's always at least one dirty bird threatening to poop on our personal parade of blessings.

· · · · · · · · · · · · · Party Poopers · · · · · · · · · · · · ·

Everyone has at least one party pooper in life—the duck we can't get in a row, the fly in our ointment, or the thorn in our flesh. Whatever we call it, it has a way of reappearing like uninvited pigeons crowding our peaceful park bench, making life difficult at best, painful at worst.

Here's a small sampling of what *it* can be:

1) A birth defect
2) A learning disability
3) A family member with an addiction
4) An estranged relationship within your family
5) Financial stress
6) A medical condition that can be managed but not cured
7) A medical diagnosis that is terminal
8) An accident that alters how you live
9) A traumatic incident that changes your life
10) A divorce you never wanted
11) A marriage that makes you want a divorce
12) A natural disaster
13) Emotional or mental instability
14) Someone who is mentally unstable who insists *you* are nuts
15) Betrayal
16) An adult child whose lifestyle is counter to your values

For reasons beyond the comprehension of even the most brilliant theologians, God chooses not to heal all that ails us physically, emotionally, or relationally—*in this lifetime.* Even those who have it all by society's standards are not exempt from debilitating or even life-threatening events—Steve Jobs, one of the most talented and wealthy men of our time, succumbed to cancer in his fifties; Arizona congresswoman Gabrielle Giffords, a woman of power and influence, received a devastating gunshot wound to her head at a campaign rally in 2011. The news is chock-full of stories of the rich and famous, their private heartaches made public.

It's against this great common denominator of pain that I become uneasy when I hear someone imply that everything can be made right in the here and now—*if only.* If only we pray harder, read the Bible more, have more faith, see the right therapist, take the right medications, read the right book, attend the right workshop, or consult the right expert. And doesn't it feel like a barrel of salt being dumped on our open wound when others make declarations of victory over the very issues from which we can't get relief?

"Our child was healed of cancer!" one rejoices, and you continue with endless rounds of chemotherapy with your very sick child.

"Our marriage was restored!" another celebrates, and you weep for the loss of connection that may never be.

"I lost twenty-five pounds!" another shouts with relief, and the only thing you've lost is count of the methods you've tried to lose even five pounds—and keep them off.

"My wayward teenager is going to Bible college!" another reports jubilantly, while your teen is awash in promiscuity and drugs.

"My adult child and I are reconciled!" another declares, and you're still reeling from the latest verbal jab that's pulsating in your gut.

During those times, it seems all we can do to utter with even a shred of honesty, "How nice for *you*."

Even the legendary composer Beethoven lacked the luxury of having everything made right in his lifetime. One morning, while making toast, I heard a gorgeous string quartet piece on the local classical station. It sent my heart soaring and my hand waving the butter knife like a conductor's baton. But as the music came to a triumphant end, the announcer said soberly, "Sadly, the composer was deaf and died before the final version of this composition debuted."

"Well, that just stinks!" I blurted out, cutting the air with an upward stroke of my knife like a ticked-off maestro. Then, approaching the stereo, I stood about a foot away and spoke directly to the announcer as if he were standing before me: "How absurd is that? Here I am in my pajamas, spreading butter on my toast, reveling in this glorious music—and the man who composed it never got to hear it."

Once again, I was confronted by the Party Pooper Factor: On one hand, most of us (Americans anyway) are blessed with relative good fortune. On the other hand, there's always *something* poised to cast a pall over our heap of happiness.

I'm not naive enough to think I can solve this complex puzzle in a three-thousand-word essay. But often it helps to acknowledge the truth about something difficult, even if we don't like what we see. Sometimes denial prevents us from breaking through to the healing power of acceptance or even triumph.

I've had to learn to live with difficult questions and less-than-satisfactory answers, because railing against them never led me to a good place. Actually, that's an understatement—railing against them led me to *dark* places in my head and heart and faith. Over time I've realized life often requires us to keep walking coura-geously through the dense fog of our doubts and fears, knowing we may not get the answers we'd hoped to find on the other side.

Mercifully, God is there to take our trembling hands, steady our wavering steps, and quiet our bewildered hearts *in spite of* incomplete answers that can't satisfy our minds.

· · · · · · · · · To Pain or Not to Pain, · · · · · · · · · · ·
That Is the Question

Not long ago, a reader-friend sent me an essay she had written after facing the life-altering party pooper of divorce. It made me think, *Which takes more faith—to have our pain removed or to trust God in spite of the pain?* (Hold that thought, and we'll take it up again shortly.)

"Suddenly Single" by Doylene Gilliland

Divorce—it's such an ugly word. The dictionary defines it as "to dissolve legally a marriage" or "to rid oneself of a spouse." See? I told you it was ugly.

I didn't ask to be divorced. I didn't really think it would ever happen. But after twenty-eight years, my dearly beloved chose to rid himself of me in order to be with another woman. And so it began. The separation of "things": his, mine, ours. Then came the legality of it all. He filed at the courthouse. I got a lawyer. He didn't want anything except his stuff, so it was pretty simple. Not that we had very much to divide. But that's not what I want to talk about. After all, stuff is just stuff.

I think I had more grief over what the divorce did to my grown children than what it did to me. I'm not sure it's any easier no matter the age. I'm grateful that I didn't have to deal with custody issues and also that my children can decide for themselves if they want a relationship with him. I just try to help keep those lines of communication open.

The day of the court hearing was the first Friday in September of 2007. My "ex" didn't appear, because he had moved two states away. My daughter, Tara, came with me because she didn't want me to be alone. I love her for that, although I think it's been harder on her than anyone else.

The proceedings were short and simple: The judge banged his gavel, declared me divorced, and wished me luck. On the way out of the courtroom, I looked at my daughter and said, "That's it? No cake? No punch? No rice throwing?" It seemed a bit of a letdown. But then again, maybe it was sadly appropriate, because that's exactly how I felt: let down. Tara decided we should have a celebratory drink at Sonic and toast our limeades to the newly unwed.

And so it came time to remove my wedding rings. I'd worn them since June 15, 1979. I love those rings. I still have them. Every once in a while when I'm going through a drawer, I run across them. I take them out and remember how excited I was when I got the engagement ring and, later, the moment the wedding band was slipped on my finger.

Single—a common word, now with a new connotation for me. Merriam-Webster defines it as "one only; individual; alone without others." Alone without others? Well, in my experience I have to strongly disagree. I have lots of others. I have way more others now than when I was married. I'm so much closer to my family than I was when married—and rightfully so. Having found myself without someone to "cleave unto," I have come to know more of my family members: nieces, nephews, aunts, uncles, sisters-in-law, brother-in-law, etc. My friends have been so good to invite me to tag along on various excursions and events, but I neither expect it nor want it all the time. Thankfully, Alone and Lonely are not identical twins—they're not even neighbors where I'm living now.

It all comes down to this: Do I like being divorced? No. Do I like being single? Yes! God has met me in so many wonderful ways in my life over the past four years. He brought people into my life whom I otherwise would never have met. I can now contemplate opportunities that I would not have otherwise out of consideration for my husband. But God is showing me that I have no limits—no strings attached. That excites me as I look forward to the next four years, and the four after that, and well, you get the picture.

So back to which takes more faith—having our party pooper plucked from our lives or trusting God in spite of its threatening presence?

On this point, it's some consolation to me when I read in the scriptures how highly God esteems *faith*. All roads in scripture, from Genesis to Revelation, keep looping back to faith. The heavy emphasis on faith is like the guy who plays a one-string banjo or infomercials that repeat the toll-free number ten times in thirty seconds: "That's 1-800-FAITH. That's right, 1-800-FAITH. Did I mention our toll free number? It's 1-800-F-A-I-T-H!"

In the book of Hebrews we read, "It's impossible to please God apart from faith" (11:6). When we hurt so bad we can't see through our tears, it may help to put that scripture in the affirmative: "Your faith pleases God." That's a power-packed truth when the resolution we have longed and prayed for is nowhere to be found. It's a truth Doylene held on to during her pain fest.

My father, a man of great faith and a diligent student of the Bible, has compassionately helped me wrestle with my own questions of why God allows heartache to run amuck. While he and I discussed the best answers to this age-old question that the likes of C. S. Lewis and Elton Trueblood could deliver, none completely satisfied my troubled soul. The concept of free will had the most helpful impact: that there is no free will without opening the door to suffering. In order to have true freedom, every person must be genuinely free—free to choose good and free to choose evil.

It's Possible to Rain on Our Own Parade

Eventually, I realized *I* had to make a choice: I could either withdraw from God or turn to Him. I decided to believe what my experience with God had taught me— *that He offers companionship in pain, not removal from pain.*

I wish it were different, because pain and suffering are the most sobering circumstances we human beings face. But making things different would be way above my pay grade. I decided to shift my thoughts to the many good things about God that I experienced and hold dear. And I began to leave unanswerable questions to a Greater Mind than mine.

After many years of walking through some dark valleys, I heartily agree with the nineteenth-century English minister Charles Spurgeon: "If an angel should fly from heaven and inform the saint personally of the Savior's love to him, the evidence would not be one whit more satisfactory than that which is borne in the heart by the Holy Ghost."

Here are a few other thoughts my Dad offered that you might find helpful as you consider your own chronic party pooper:

1) *Am I a Party Pooper?* It's good to sort through the question as to whether *we* are the primary cause of our misery—or someone else's. A good friend, mentor, or counselor can help us work through some things that might be our own doing and help us visualize a change that is possible.

2) *God: The Celestial Party Pooper?* It's good to remember that God is never the source of our pain. While it's hard for us to fathom, a distinction can be made between allowing something to happen and causing it to happen.

3) *Party Pooping Happens.* It's best to find a way to deal with misery-making circumstances in the most positive way we can. The alternative is to become bitter, depressed, and self-absorbed.

Sometimes it's not necessarily a miracle we need (though it would seem deliriously helpful) but a miraculous shift in perspective instead. This can be a type of "virtual miracle" that helps us better cope with our party pooping experiences. We may just find that our happiness does not have to be put on hold after all.

I have a friend whose sister was diagnosed with borderline personality disorder. In a nutshell, she has a relational tendency to bite the hand that helps her. After my friend had courageously extended her hand many times to her sister, only to keep drawing it back with teeth marks, she thought, *Is it possible that I could be happy if my sister remains a mess the rest of her life?* And in a miracle moment, the answer came to her, *Yes. Yes I can. I can drop my expectations and accept what is. I can entrust her to God and stop trying to play God in her life.*

My friend initiated boundaries to protect her mind and heart from her sister's periodic ranting and verbal assaults. Then she began to try loving her sister for who she is, not for who she hoped her sister would be. "My sister has not changed, but I have," my friend told me. "I don't expect this world or the people who inhabit it to be perfect—*that* would be heaven. And this world is so not heaven."

As we face our nagging party pooping problems—if we have only the tiniest bit of hope—may we find the courage to ask God for a miracle shift in perspective. And may He bring bits of heaven to us by replacing our troubled thoughts with His peace.

Even when our circumstances don't change, we can.

Hope is the feeling that the feeling
you have isn't permanent.[2]

JEAN KERR

. . . .

A man should look for what is,
and not for what he thinks should be.[3]

ALBERT EINSTEIN

. . . .

*I'm glad in God, far happier than you
would ever guess. . . . Actually, I don't a
sense of needing anything personally.
I've learned by now to be quite content
whatever my circumstances. I'm just as
happy with little as with much, with much
as with little. I've found the recipe for being
happy whether full or hungry, hands full or
hands empty. Whatever I have, wherever I
am, I can make it through anything in the
One who makes me who I am.*

PHILIPPIANS 4:10–13

Reflections on Your Well-Lived Laugh—
Designing a Life That Keeps You Smiling

1) On a scale of 1 (being lowest) to 10 (the highest), how much does the pressure to fix "it" bother you?

2) What are two or three words that describe how you feel about this pressure now?

3) What are two or three words that describe how you would feel if this pressure were lessened or removed?

4) Looking at your answers 1–3, on a scale of 1 to 10, how motivated are you to reduce this pressure?

5) Who is someone with whom you feel emotionally safe—who will encourage you while you decide how best to reduce this pressure?

6) Use this space to write some thoughts or feelings that this pressure has brought to your mind.

7) If this pressure negatively impacts your life in a significant way, try finishing this sentence:
I want to live well, laugh often, and smile more! I can begin by choosing to take this one step. . .

11
Rock Star Moms

❧

The Pressure to Make
Something of Yourself

Thanks in part to the Women's Movement of the '70s, females today have many more options for how to spend their lives. Personally, I love the opportunities available to us. I have found myself on many occasions admiring (okay, *envying*) the gifts of other women—from the right-brained artist to the left-brained chemist. Recently, it dawned on me that there is an entire "world within" *every* woman that reflects God's brilliance.

But if you're a mom, balancing many things at once can require the multitasking prowess of a Barnum and Bailey plate spinner. For women who relish "being busy," that's just the cherry on the big top—they love the sense of accomplishment that comes with a job well done on many fronts. For others, especially moms who work full-time, the days can be *too* full—making them feel as if they've been roped into a perpetual three-ring circus.

After that common experience that so many women share—giving birth to a first child—I remember how suddenly chaotic my once-ordered world became. While I had a love affair with slumber, Baby Trevor was allergic to sleep. One restless week in, I found myself sitting in bed with a set of fire-engine-red mammary glands pulsating with pain. It was as if my breasts had taken on a life of their own—the way your arm takes a vacation from your body when you fall asleep on it. The appendage becomes impervious to any effort to move it, having lost all feeling.

But I could feel my breasts all right—it was like someone had lit charcoal briquettes and placed them in my nursing bra.

Tears trickling down my cheeks, I called a friend who had given birth to her firstborn son, Alex, a few months earlier.

"Sally," I squeaked, my voice barely audible from sheer exhaustion, "why didn't you tell me this was so hard?"

There was a long pause on the other end of the line while I cried softly. "Oh, Rachel, I'm so sorry," my friend consoled. "I didn't have the heart to tell you. I thought maybe it wouldn't be as hard for you as it was for me."

This is generally true of motherhood: No one has the heart to tell you how hard it can be. Or maybe they assume other women are handling it better than they are. But since those distant mammaries, um. . . memories, of adjusting to a newborn, I've done a lot of talking to moms. The reality is most of us are pedaling as fast as we can to—as we say in the Mom-Army—"be all we must be." You know: employee, entrepreneur, driver, chef, tutor, and all-around Proverbs 31 woman (who some women try to emulate while others would like to have her stricken from the biblical record, or just stricken in general).

And forget spending time with a good book, a good friend, or good grief. . .*alone*. What about exercising? Most women I know have to get up very early in the morning to pull those Lycra shorts out of their magic aprons. I applaud them—with golf claps from underneath my pillows and quilts, warmly tucked in bed.

Me And My Papparazzi

Author Anne Morrow Lindbergh wrote that the multitasking wife and mother is like the center of a wheel with spokes going out in all directions. I think that's a perfect word picture for today's nest nurturer. Though sometimes I feel like those spokes are poking *inward*, like an entourage of porcupines needling me to meet their many needs.

If you're a mom raising small children, this may very well be the most energy-sapping period of your life. Babies, toddlers, and preschoolers require a tremendous amount of time as well as physical and emotional stamina. Moms with older children and teens know that developing character in their kids takes special vigilance—and keeping up with extracurricular activities can require these parents to morph into scheduling geniuses with chauffeur's licenses.

Even if you don't have children, you're probably working, volunteering, or taking care of aging family members—and the relentless need-meeting can leave you on the verge of mental vertigo (or at least in need of some alone time with a pastry case).

Then, into this maelstrom of activity and responsibility, some of us add one more zinger of pressure to bat around in our heads: I need to *make* something of myself.

Why, when many of us receive ample appreciation from family and friends, do we feel the need to be "a woman of influence"? Why this pressure when we have only vestiges of spare time? I'm not completely sure. The reasons probably vary from woman to woman.

Certainly, some women *don't* struggle with this particular pressure. A friend once told me, "I love being a homemaker. I love being available to family and friends and keeping house and cooking. Frankly, I love the freedom." Hear, hear! I agree—with everything except the keeping house and cooking part. Call me old-fashioned, but I miss the good old days of butlers and maids.

For the women I know who work by necessity rather than choice—including single moms—this pressure can still be relentless. Yet the sheer logistics of "pursuing a passion" are immense—when it's hard enough to find margin to apply mascara.

Sometimes it feels like Sam I Am is stuck in your head asking a litany of annoying but important questions: *Can you do more? Can you do it with a job? With three kids? With a dog?* You may well be able to do "more" if that's your passion. But pacing yourself may be key to saving your sanity—and keeping your hair from looking as if it's been styled in Whoville.

I admit that I'm among the ranks of those who hope I have something valuable to offer my fellow man *in addition to* being a homemaker and raising good kids. (Hope springs eternal.) I like the feeling of using my God-given gifts to lighten the load of others.

It bears saying, though, that we can get into trouble if we fall into the comparison trap, constantly sizing up *our* gifts against someone else's—and deciding we're coming up short. And then there's the sticky wicket of driving ourselves to exhaustion by trying to validate our existence through achievements that perhaps God has not called us to.

Here's something that can prove helpful in

developing and pursuing our gifts: knowing whether we tend to be a do-er or be-er—or even a do-be-do-be-do-er, vacillating between doing and being. Typically, I avoid generalizations because they can oversimplify complex issues. But for our purposes here, I offer you "A Tale of Two Moms"—one a be-er, the other a do-er, and their quests to deal with the pressure to make something of themselves.

· · · · · · · · · · · · Rachel, the Be-er · · · · · · · · · · · ·

In this achievement-admiring, responsibility-loving society, it makes me nervous to confess to being more of a be-er. Be-er sounds, well, lazy. And it *can* be if I lose track of time being contemplative or relational and leave my house in shambles. But be-ers can actually be respectable conservationists. We have a knack for saving time and energy (sometimes even money), because before we dive into anything, we side-tracking be-ers contemplate pivotal questions like:

1) Is this really necessary?
2) Is there a quicker way to do this?
3) Does this fit the priorities in my life?

(A friend who helped edit this manuscript wrote in the margin, "Where were you with these questions when I agreed to host six couples and babysit their four kids for five hours the evening before having my own kids and grandkids over for Sunday lunch?")

See? Be-ers can be very helpful. But timing is everything.

I must confess that I reached a point when I wanted to do a bit more with my life. Despite my knack for asking questions that lead to lightbulb moments, I realized Oprah's job was already taken. So, being a deep thinker and encourager by nature, I dabbled in the writing world to see if God might use those gifts in that field.

My writing dream began percolating in my brain about sixteen years ago. A young editor at *Better Homes and Gardens* liked a zany travel story I'd submitted and offered me an assignment on garden tours. Never mind that I hadn't nurtured anything green to life except a lima bean in a plastic cup during kindergarten—I was on the case.

I dived in full throttle, taking copious notes as I traipsed through mind-blowing English gardens and topiaries, and reported the flowers and events of my trip with my trademark offbeat observations. I turned in my first draft and was almost fired full throttle. Somehow I missed the directive to write the article in a just-the-facts sort of way.

Since that time, I've written professionally for various book projects and had two of my own books of offbeat devotions published. Though all of these experiences were rewarding, none of them was easy. Early on, to meet a deadline, I had to type with one hand while holding a nursing a baby in my other arm. Another time I wrote under the inspiration of a sinus infection radiating through every cavity in my head. So much for working in trendy cafés with tulip-filled window boxes.

Then there are the inevitable head battles. Even yesterday I was thinking, *My cat can write better than this. A three-year-old can write better than this.* Anybody *can write better than this—I'm going to have to return the royalty advance.* I spied Whitney chewing a piece of gum from a pack purchased that morning and quipped, "Spit that out— everything's going back to Walmart. Mommy can't write jack squat." A cup of coffee later, having wrangled some lame sentences into respectable ones, I looked up from the keyboard and sheepishly told my husband, "Maybe I overreacted."

As a be-er, I will always be grateful that writing has

allowed me to make a modest but helpful income from the comfort of my home and favorite coffee shops. Yet I still feel the allure of an even simpler life with fewer commitments, one that cuts down on mother-guilt.

You see, my contemplative nature comes in handy if I have to write an article about "living in the moment." It's less handy when I've become so lost in the moment that I look up from my computer to see four vaguely familiar people asking me in unison monotone, "Where's dinner?" You can see how this dynamic complicates life at our house, keeping me in the doghouse whenever I have writing work.

So, that's me. Let me introduce you to a do-er friend of mine.

・・・・・・・・・・・ Jennifer, the Do-er ・・・・・・・・・・・

Jennifer Sanchez is one of those women who enjoys a sense of accomplishment from managing a full life well—she's a vocalist, voice teacher, wife, and mother. Jenn became my walking buddy, and through our jaunts I got to know her as a bubbly, down-to earth, baseball cap-and-shorts-wearing mom by day and opera aficionado by night.

One day Jenn invited me to hear her sing at a small church. As I sat in the pew, her rich soprano voice resonated within the walls of the tiny sanctuary, filling my entire being with emotion. Though she sang in Italian, German, and French—and I understood not a word—I was moved to tears. It was as if the compelling instrument of her voice transported me to some centuries-old, ivy-covered, stone cathedral at evensong. During intermission, I sat in quiet awe. I thought, *My walking buddy really is a professional opera singer.*

Afterwards, I met Jennifer for dinner at a cozy restaurant. As we sat back in cushy brown suede chairs, I felt like there was an entire musical world inside my friend—that I'd had just a small glimpse of what was there. I wanted to know more.

"Give me the highlights," I urged as I settled in with a cup of chamomile tea.

"Let's see," she answered. "I've sung the roles of Donna Anna, Violetta, and the title role in *Madame Butterfly* in various places around the country and Europe. I even once won a five-thousand-dollar prize at a competition."

Jenn smiled pensively. "But my career had to be put on hold when my first child, Nathaniel, was born. I remember thinking, *This mom thing is a lot harder than I thought it would be—what now?* When Sophia was born less than two years later, I had the answer to that question: 'Now the goose is cooked.' "

I laughed out loud. So much for the calming properties of chamomile.

That was a feeling I knew well. "So what happened after you had *two* little ones?"

"I was unprepared for what I was facing—I had invested heavily in a career, and now I had a family that meant the world to me. There was still the flicker of a diva somewhere deep inside me, but my body—my instrument—had taken a hit. I was a little depressed and felt trapped in motherhood."

Jenn then explained how she and her husband devised a way for her to spend time, periodically, in New York where she would study with a world-renowned voice teacher. But Jennifer's career really began to bounce back after she was offered a contract to sing with the Florida Orchestra. She now sings with the Dallas Symphony Chorus. "It's been hard," she said, "but God has given me the motivation and support to manage a family and career."

What's a mother to do when she is called to be a mom *and* called to share a gift with the world outside her home? One mom, whose children are now grown, offered me this advice:

You really can have it all. Just usually not all at once. I encourage women to tend their dream in small doses. That is, you can "start" and feed that passion of yours by, say, writing a blog, taking a class or two—perhaps even online, creating a web page, or working part-time. Then you can let your dream-calling-career grow as your children do.

One thing is sure: If you find yourself battling thoughts that you are "not enough" rather than feeling inspired to "make something of yourself," that's not coming from a good place. God motivates through encouragement, not condemnation.

And I don't know if you've noticed this, but God rarely seems to be in a rush. It's like He's caught up in a time continuum of eternity or something. So take a page from His playbook and consider a leisurely pace if that works for you.

For women who juggle so much need-meeting for others, spend some time taking care of yourself. Slow down a bit. By so doing, you'll give God space to speak and yourself the chance to listen. Let's allow Him to lead our unique be-er or do-er or do-be-do-be-do-er personalities into that beautiful place where our giftedness meets a true need in the world—or the neighborhood.

One last note about time: While *carpe diem* has an inspiring ring to it, the vast majority of us live life as a marathon, not a sprint. If you have the option to "make something of yourself" little by little, it's really okay to take the tortoise approach for a season. Then, when your kids are more independent, you can get your hare on, baby!

Go confidently in the
direction of your dreams![1]

HENRY DAVID THOREAU

. . . .

We all have dreams. But in order to
make dreams come into reality, it takes
an awful lot of determination, dedication,
self-discipline, and effort.[2]

JESSE OWENS

Reflections on Your Well-Lived Laugh—
Designing a Life That Keeps You Smiling

1) On a scale of 1 (being lowest) to 10 (the highest), how much does the pressure to make something of yourself bother you?

2) What are two or three words that describe how you feel about this pressure now?

3) What are two or three words that describe how you would feel if this pressure were lessened or removed?

4) Looking at your answers 1–3, on a scale of 1 to 10, how motivated are you to reduce this pressure?

5) Who is someone with whom you feel emotionally safe—who will encourage you while you decide how best to reduce this pressure?

6) Use this space to write some thoughts or feelings that this pressure has brought to your mind.

7) If this pressure negatively impacts your life in a significant way, try finishing this sentence:
I want to live well, laugh often, and smile more! I can begin by choosing to take this one step. . .

12

Best Fits

❖

The Pressure to Do It All

At a point during the hectic holiday season, I suddenly felt the need for a little quiet reflection (and a caffeine boost) before the arrival of guests. So I lovingly reached for my upper of choice: a bag of coffee beans. As I held the soft, bumpy bag in my hand, my eyes fell on several symbols imploring me to save things—from the rain forest in Africa to the sea turtles in the Atlantic.

In that tired, overwhelmed moment, the thing that most needed saving was *me*. Without proper caffeination—trust me—no manner of marine life would *want* my help. And I thought, *Could I just have a simple cup of coffee without thinking about saving something or someone right now?* I don't mean to sound cranky—or heaven forbid, uncaring—but it just seems lately I can't gargle mouthwash or sip a cup of coffee without feeling a little bit, sometimes a lotta bit, of tension. And often that tension is directed inward: *Oh my goodness, I should be saving something.* "Hey kids, get my leotards and cape—stat!"

I don't know about you, but some days, if my flip-flops match and my kids arrive at school relatively on time, that's about as much responsibility as I can muster. As the saying goes, "Life happens." And some days—or seasons—it's about all we can do to keep our sanity, faith, and family intact. So while I'm warm to finding a helping niche, I'm lukewarm to having someone else define what that is *for* me.

In a culture where there are no less than three (often as many as six) planet-saving, socially responsible icons on just about every product I purchase, how do I balance my need for occasional disconnect to reorient the compass of my life? And further, how do I decide what's most deserving of my limited time, energy, and resources?

Even more importantly, how do I tamp down the guilt that threatens to engulf my conscience every time I say no to the good that's bound to happen if only I would "do my part"?

• • • • • • • • • • • Save. . .Your Sanity • • • • • • • • • •

Let's face it, appearing uncaring is a big no-no these days—there are lots of needs out there, and it's our job to fill them all. Or at least that's how it feels. Knowing "when to say *when*" to all the voices calling to us is key if we don't want *our* face to appear as the symbol for the next big social initiative: Save the Burned-Out Woman.

Beyond social issues, many women feel the pressure of whatever currently defines the Ideal Woman. We all know instinctively this woman is fiction, but we all feel the occasional heat to measure up to her—which can make us a real piece of business.

Here's a small list of some pressures that go through our heads, contributed by a Real Woman who prefers to go by the name Deep Throat (I mean, Anonymous):

1. Pressure to have it all, but not act like you *want* to have it all—because that would appear materialistic.
1. Pressure to be fun—the life of the party—but not a stumbling block. After all, one must be sensitive to proprieties.
2. Pressure to have a clean house, make organic meals, be a fashionista with nonchipping nails—and make it look effortless.
3. Pressure to be "well-endowed" but not admit to having surgery to get the look.
4. Pressure to nurse because that's what the good moms do—even though after a few babies that can lead to pressure #4.
5. Pressure to be more spiritual by having better time with God than others but sharing it as being transparent.
6. Pressure to cut coupons and pinch pennies because that's what responsible wives do.
7. Pressure to modify your children's bad behavior

in public, but act as if you're concerned with their heart (when all you really want is for the tantrum to stop—"This instant!"—and peace to return to the sandbox).

8. Pressure to be very involved in ministry that has a "high impact"—because it sounds better than "low impact" and you get a free Under Armor stretchy shirt with a cool logo.

I was talking to my friend Laura when the subject of head games came up. Laura knew all too well how do-it-all burnout can lead to "I-give-up" meltdown, having had her emotional eyebrows singed some years back.

I'm eight years older than Laura, and if I hadn't had two "surprise" babies late in life, it's likely she and I would never have connected. Ironically, self-imposed pressure to measure up almost kept me from a long-term friendship that has brought much joy to my life. I remember when I first saw Laura, while picking up my kids from the megachurch preschool.

At a glance, I could see that she was everything I wasn't. And some things I envied. And well, if I could just avoid eye contact, I wouldn't have to feel "less" than and hold an actual conversation with her. Laura At-a-Glance was young, pretty, blond, and fit, and she wore pastel cotton fabrics that were perfectly "broken in." Plus, there were the hip shoes—a stylish combination of canvas and rubber that no doubt cost a small fortune at REI.

I made a quick mental note: *High achiever. Probable former homecoming queen. Avoid at all costs.*

There I was, child in arms, outfitted in an extra-large Shrek T-shirt from a recent trip to Universal Studios. I was just about to make a quick exit when I heard someone call out, "Are you Rachel St. John-Gilbert?" I turned around.

Guess who was walking down the red carpet (I mean hallway) toward me, looking way too cool for my comfort.

I was trapped. Without time to apply Chapstick or run a comb through my hair, I forced a smile. Imagine my surprise when she asked if I would be willing to give a talk to the Mother of Preschoolers (MOPs) group at the church. She was smiley and nice and seemed intrigued that I'd written a quirky book, all things that made me feel better about myself. Since feeling better about myself is often in short supply, I thought, *Gee, maybe this might work after all.*

Many years later, I'm still trapped by Laura. Only now, it's more like captured by how comfortable I am in her presence—no mental gymnastics of sifting words or motives when we're together. After spending time with her, I always come away feeling more aware of God's goodness and less aware of my badness.

Okay, I admit I was a bad judge of character initially—but those shoes of hers really threw me. However, my first impressions hadn't been completely off. Laura was indeed a high achiever who for a time had found emotional safety in meeting cultural expectations.

"I was always striving to be the perfect Christian, wife, and mother—and have the perfect body," she eventually confided to me. "As long as I kept all those things going, I felt good about myself."

But it wasn't long after we met that Laura's ability to "do it all" began to wane. She and her husband, Jeff, were in their early thirties, the parents of three children. Jeff, who looks like he is related to Dwayne "The Rock" Johnson, was coaching middle school football and basketball.

"Here I had these amazing children," he once told me, "and I would leave for work before they woke up and get home after they were asleep."

Jeff and Laura eventually decided to open a franchise specializing in children's fitness. What could be better than working together, staying fit, including their kids in their work, and. . .making lots of money?

But the story that begins well goes south faster than an Olympic bobsled team.

The family needed an income during the start-up phase of their business, so Jeff worked full-time as an area director for Young Life Ministries. He also taught Sunday school for young married couples. Laura was raising three small children and was involved in leadership with MOPs.

With little free time, they began to feel the pressure of too many folks and too many needs. Jeff and Laura were soon depleted from trying to meet them all.

And the work was much greater than they had anticipated. "The monotony of being in charge of every minute detail at the gym began to take its toll," Laura recalls. To make matters worse, the nation's economy began a downward turn. Before long, the couple realized the only way out pointed to crippling financial loss.

"We were the proverbial frogs in the pot of water," said Laura. "We were approaching the boiling point before we knew what hit us—and we realized we weren't doing anything that really mattered most to us."

As the stress mounted, Laura turned to a comforting

old friend from her past: who goes by the name of Food. (Maybe you know Food? I know it all too well.) But gaining weight was incompatible with Laura's high standards for herself. So she made a simple adjustment: What went down had to come up. This dangerous arrangement was obviously at odds with the perfect image Laura had been striving to achieve.

"I was at the end of myself," she says. "I knew I needed help, but felt I didn't deserve it—even from God."

Enter Jeff, who stepped in to take charge like any coach whose team is being routed.

"We can't control a lot of things right now," he told Laura, "but we can *struggle well* by focusing on our health and our relationship with the Lord." Slowly but steadily the dominoes in the couple's lives began to fall their way.

"After two years of painstaking therapy, God set me free from the addiction to food," she now says with confidence. Soon after that, Laura gave birth to a fourth child and the family sold their house. Selling the business was a more arduous trek, ultimately completed at a loss.

Since that time, Laura and Jeff have forged new priorities that fit them like a glove. They now attend a smaller church where they feel refreshed rather than pressured. They host a Bible study in their home for young couples who have become like family to their children. They coach their kids' soccer teams. Laura is taking classes to complete her master's degree in counseling.

"It will take about *forever* to complete my degree," she jokes, "but I'm passionate about marriage and families."

Laura's advice to women who feel pressure to "do everything"?

1. Nurture your family first.
2. Ask God want He wants your priorities to be—and don't take on more than that.
3. Add margin to your life. The unexpected happens more often than we expect (thus the term unexpected)—so allow space to handle those surprises well.

· · · · · · · · · · · What's Your Best Fit? · · · · · · · · · · ·

We all know how hard it is to sift through endless ministries and causes to determine those that are a best fit for us. With a click of a button, we can now access detailed information about gaping holes of human need in every corner of the world. To figure out which ones God is calling *us* to help alleviate, we can ask ourselves, "What was I created to do? What makes me feel God's pleasure when I do it?"

It may take some time to sort this out. We may not know what our best fits are until we try on a few hats. Inevitably though, we'll find that best fits *energize* us while other things deplete us. And best fits allow us to maintain our commitment to our spouse and family as well.

Homing in on best fits can be complicated by a newish phenomenon I call "extreme Christianity." Maybe it's just the glossy photos of men with three-day shadows, shaved heads, and tattoos that grace so many Christian magazines—but there's a not-so-subtle message out there that unless you're the spiritual equivalent to a bungee-jumping adrenaline junkie with a savior complex, you're an ineffective Christian nerd. If you're not willing to live at the poverty level and tithe the remainder of your income, or spend your vacations in a third world country, or live greener than Kermit the Frog. . .you're just a poser, not a player. This pressure can lead us to poor decisions based on guilt and societal pressure rather than on the voice of God and our unique gifts.

When I talk with older Christians about these more ardent perspectives, they often say, "There's nothing *new* under the sun." The trends may seem different, but on further scrutiny, they are essentially the same. The realization got me wondering if this emphasis on extreme, high-impact Christianity wasn't all that different from works-based theology—which has been around since the time of Paul. You know, that stuff he warned against so strongly in the book of Galatians.

Please understand: *My intention is not to diminish the service of Christians who have been called by God to personally take the gospel to people in dire circumstances, whether in the United States or around the globe.* Rather, my goal is to point out that if we're involved in high-impact ministries that are a poor fit for us, *we* are the ones who stand to be impacted. And we can find ourselves blindsided, benched from the game of life, watching from the sidelines as we ice down the injuries that come with emotional, spiritual, and physical depletion. That doesn't make us much good to anyone or any cause, no matter how critical the need.

In the tiniest nutshell, I am saying that *people have limits based on their God-given personality, intellect, and physiology, and on where they are in their spiritual walk at any given time.* Authors Bob and Joel Kilpatrick put it this way in *The Art of Being You:*

Every canvas has a border. . .we are created to be great in spite of, and even because of, our limitations. God has expressed Himself uniquely in each of us, and He uses our limitations to bring glory to himself.

Much of the art of finding best fits has to do with our present season of life. Tending new marriages, nurturing young children, and building careers can be some of the most intensive endeavors we undertake—so those seasons may not be conducive to volunteering large amounts of our time, resources, and energy.

Perhaps the times of single- or empty-nested-ness provide some of us more latitude for spiritual exploration—like taking mission trips to remote parts of the world or making unconventional, even radical lifestyle changes.

If God is calling you, no matter the season, by all means heed His voice. If, however, your spouse disputes whether you truly heard the voice of God telling you to move the family to Africa, you may want to employ the services of an arbitrator before leaving. Otherwise your mate may be more than willing to pack your bags for you.

In the final analysis, how we choose to spend our lives and express our devotion to Jesus Christ is a very personal matter. It requires taking many things and people into account. But if we're not careful in this age of information overload and high-tech marketing, we can find ourselves living the priorities of others—not the ones God has called us to live. That's just a little something to keep in mind the next time someone insinuates you're sitting on your laurels and you need to get off your duff and jump on their bandwagon.

Jeff and Laura learned the hard way that people aren't designed to "do it all." Take it from Coach Jacobs: You are less likely to burn out if you pace yourself and invest in those things that are God's best fits for *you*.

He is a wise man who wastes no energy
on pursuits for which he is not fitted;
and he is wiser still who from among
the things he can do well, chooses and
resolutely follows the best.[1]

WILLIAM GLADSTONE
BRITISH PRIME MINISTER

. . . .

Devoting a little of yourself to
everything means committing a
great deal of yourself to nothing.[2]

MICHAEL LEBOEF

. . . .

Time is the most valuable coin in your life.
You. . .determine how that coin will be
spent. Be careful that you do not let
other people spend it for you.[3]

CARL SANDBURG

Reflections on Your Well-Lived Laugh—
Designing a Life That Keeps You Smiling

1) On a scale of 1 (being lowest) to 10 (the highest), how much does the pressure to do it all bother you?

2) What are two or three words that describe how you feel about this pressure now?

3) What are two or three words that describe how you would feel if this pressure were lessened or removed?

4) Looking at your answers 1–3, on a scale of 1 to 10, how motivated are you to reduce this pressure?

5) Who is someone with whom you feel emotionally safe—who will encourage you while you decide how best to reduce this pressure?

6) Use this space to write some thoughts or feelings that this pressure has brought to your mind.

7) If this pressure negatively impacts your life in a significant way, try finishing this sentence:

I want to live well, laugh often, and smile more! I can begin by choosing to take this one step. . .

Epilogue

Own It. Work It.

I think the first half of life is about trying on lots of hats, The second half is about wearing those hats that feel like they were tailor-made for you by a milliner. As you begin to develop your own unique perspective—and own it—you learn how to really *rock those hats*!

Owning your own perspective is freedom—freedom from feeling trapped by a point of view that fits your grown-up head like a baby's bonnet. Though we can't cherry-pick the things that happen to us in life, we are *always* free to choose a perspective that works for us. As the saying goes, *Pain is inevitable, but misery is optional.*

Psychiatrists say that the issue underlying depression is that of feeling trapped, without choices, stuck in a no-win situation. Developing our own perspective empowers us to choose the *attitudes* that make our challenges more tolerable—sometimes even surmountable.

I promised myself that I would not invoke the name of the legendary concentration camp survivor and Austrian psychologist Dr. Viktor Frankl because he is so widely quoted, perhaps overquoted—but with good reason. Having come to the end of our one-sided discussions about the pressures we battle in our heads, I find my thoughts turning to Dr. Frankl's book, *Man's Search for Meaning*. If you ever feel hopelessly trapped in an unpleasant circumstance ,this book offers virtually instant perspective. He writes, "Everything can be taken from a man [or a woman] but one thing: the last of human freedoms—to choose one's attitude in any given set of circumstances, to choose one's own way." Considering the suffering and indignities this man endured, that's one powerful statement.

Christians aren't immune from feeling trapped, and we don't possess a "Get out of jail free" pass. Like our secular counterparts, we, too, can readily hand over our freedom—the freedom to choose our own way—to those we fear will disapprove, belittle, or even dismiss us. It takes courage to become a WOP (Woman of Perspective) and boldly yet graciously wear the hats that make us feel smashing and confident—like Katherine Hepburn in a fedora.

Let's remember the liberating words of the apostle Paul: "Christ has set us free to live a free life. So take your stand! Never again let anyone put a harness of slavery on you" (Galatians 5:1). Away with that harness! Open that cell door! Take ownership of your perspective! And—with God's help—design a life that keeps you smiling, one choice at a time.

As for me, at midlife I realize I thrive best with lots of margin in my days—time for hanging out with my family, time to get a good night's rest, time to explore quaint and unique places, and time with a few connecty friends who want to know and be fully known.

Right now I am not personally called to visit a need-riddled continent, or save spotted creatures (why are the spotted ones always endangered?), or even recycle resources like plastic baggies. (Though my Depression-reared mother washes and reuses them.)

I am learning to applaud the passions of others without, at the same time, disparaging my own—even if they seem "low impact" by comparison. And mostly, they do.

Honestly, I still feel conflicted about writing professionally, precisely because it encroaches on the margin I love so much. What I *do* feel called to is encouraging my fellow female sojourners in their Christian faith—whether that's in the foxhole with a few heaven-sent friends or in the bunker with my ten-year-old relic of a laptop, tapping out the contents of my brain and heart in chapter form.

So it's time to say, "So long," and leave you to *your* thoughts. May you be emboldened to try on those hats that call your name, even if your critics click their tongues with nay-saying or wag their index fingers in disapproval. Even if those critics are your own thoughts.

When you find yourself boldly rocking that headgear that fits, might I be the first to say, "Hat's off to you!"

The real voyage of discovery consists not in seeking new landscapes, but in having new eyes.[1]
MARCEL PROUST

Acknowledgments

Becky Johnson—This book wouldn't be here if it weren't for you. After all the handholding you've done on this manuscript, you probably wish you'd kept your mouth shut. You are the most gifted, fascinating, bighearted person I know. It means the world to me that I can count on you when I need help of any kind. Thank you from the bottom of my heart for taking time from your loco life to put your remarkable imprint on this manuscript. What I've most wanted is to offer a message that's encouraging and entertaining. Life is hard, and I hope we've made it a tad easier for some women—at least for a little while.

Greg Johnson—A good man and a great agent. Thank you for taking care of Becky. And thank you for taking care of business.

Ruth Ann Arnold (Mom)—You are amazing at turns of phrase, dialogue, and other editing miracles that do not come naturally to me. Thank you for the considerable number of hours you gave freely and joyously for the sake of this manuscript and my sanity. I think you may have saved both.

George Arnold (Dad)—Thank you for taking care of Mom and encouraging her as she was encouraging me. And thank you, too, for offering insights and sending affirmation when I really needed a boost. When I think back to the fireside chats we had about the meaning of life beginning when I was about five, I realize some things never change.

Scott, Trevor, Tori, and Whitney—Thank you for holding down the fort (and sweeping its floors and laying in supplies) when I needed writing time. I know we are all dancing a jig now that I'm *done*. Thank you for making my ordinary days extraordinary. I love how much we laugh together and how much we love and support each other.

Paul Muckley—Thank you for being a genuinely nice guy who is very easy to work with. You did an excellent job spearheading (a nice, manly verb) this project.

Laura Jacobs, Jennifer Sanchez, Katy Boldroff, Lynn Morrissey—thank you for being interviewees, sounding boards, and even editors at critical junctures for important concepts and chapters.

Lisa Sachse—Thank you for being so accommodating to me and my girls on the tail end of this project when we needed it most. We are so blessed to have you and Lindy and Haley in our lives.

Almond Tree Studio—Thank you Bob Almond for racing to the park "in twenty" to shoot my mug shot when I created my own photo emergency. I guess marketing really needed a picture after all. Sue, thank you for holding the bunny up to make me smile and Photoshopping out all the visible flaws. Thank you, Scott, for having friends who bail me out of tight spots.

Notes

Introduction
1. Stephen R. Covey, *The 7 Habits of Highly Effective People* (New York: Free Press, 1989, 2004).
2. Dan Baker, Ph.D., *What Happy People Know* (New York: St. Martin's, 2003).
3. B. F. Johnson, as shared via e-mail.

Chapter 1
1. Leo Rosten, *Leo Rosten's Carnival of Wit* (New York: Penguin, 1994).
2. Ibid.
3. Ibid.

Chapter 2
1. www.quotesea.com (accessed February 16, 2012).
2. www.theideahive.com, (accessed February 16, 2012).

Chapter 3
1. Leo Rosten, *Leo Rosten's Carnival of Wit* (New York: Penguin, 1994).
2. Ibid.

Chapter 4
1. Becky Freeman, *Real Magnolias* (Nashville: Thomas Nelson, 1999).
2. www.word-gems.com, (accessed February 16, 2012).

Chapter 5
1. www.drbenkim.com (accessed February 16, 2012).
2. Thane Peterson, "Julia Child: A Little Bit of Everything and Have a Good Time," *Bloomberg Businessweek* November 12, 2000.
3. Martha Hawkins, *Finding Martha's Place* (New York: Touchstone, 2010).

4. www.longevity.about.com (accessed February 16, 2012).
Leo Rosten, *Leo Rosten's Carnival of Wit* (New York: Penguin, 1994).
Ibid.

Chapter 6
1. www.inspirational-quotes.info (accessed February 16, 2012).
2. Ibid.

Chapter 7
1. Leo Rosten, *Leo Rosten's Carnival of Wit* (New York: Penguin, 1994.
2. Ibid.

Chapter 8
1. www.theopedia.com (accessed February 16, 2012).
2. Becky Freeman, *Real Magnolias* (Nashville: Thomas Nelson, 1999).
3. www.quoteland.com (accessed February 16, 2012).

Chapter 9
1. Becky Freeman, *Real Magnolias* (Nashville: Thomas Nelson, 1999).
2. Ibid.

Chapter 10
1. Charles Spurgeon,
2. Leo Rosten, *Leo Rosten's Carnival of Wit* (New York: Penguin Books, 1994).
3. Ibid.

Chapter 11
1. www.quoteland.com (accessed February 16, 2012).
2. www.brainyquote.com (accessed February 27, 2012).

Chapter 12
1. John Maxwell, *Today Matters* (New York: Warner Faith, 2004).
2. Ibid.
3. Ibid.

Epilogue
1. www.brainyquote.com (accessed February 16, 2012).